"Prayer is a particular kind of relation
By examining the fundamentals of tha.
who we are—with straightforward Bible exposition, William Fппп
helps you understand and enter into it."
    Timothy J. Keller, Pastor, Redeemer Presbyterian Church,
    New York City; best-selling author, *The Reason for God*

"There are not many books on prayer, and there are fewer good books
on prayer. Here is a handbook on the subject that combines clarity
and brevity and provides us with a thoroughly biblical and understandable framework for prayer. I commend it enthusiastically."
    Alistair Begg, Senior Pastor, Parkside Church, Cleveland, Ohio

"Philip grounds prayer in the nature of the triune God, thus avoid-
ing the modern evangelical tendency to make 'the experience of
prayer' central. When divine Sonship and not feelings define you,
then you have real prayer with a real God. This book will bless you."
    Paul E. Miller, Director, seeJesus; author, *A Praying Life* and
    A Loving Life

"This book made me want to pray! It shows us what God is like—a
Father who speaks, and whose adopted children are able to speak to
him, by his Spirit. It is thoroughly biblical, honest, and entertaining.
Philip takes our eyes off ourselves and our performance and onto
God—Father, Son, and Spirit."
    Caz Dodds, Scotland Assistant Team Leader, UCCF

"Wonderfully refreshing, biblically realistic, and personally moti-
vational—this book cuts through the stereotypes and guilt about
prayer and presents us with our amazing privileges. It will do your
heart good!"
    David Jackman, Former President, Proclamation Trust,
    London

"To speak freshly about prayer is neither easy nor common. Philip has done it here. In answering so well the big question he has set himself, he has enriched my thinking and practice."

Dick Lucas, Rector Emeritus, St. Helen's Church, Bishopsgate, United Kingdom; Founder, Proclamation Trust

"In this wonderful book I find that my prayer life needs a reality check. The heart of prayer is not only talking *to* God but knowing I pray because God is a speaking God."

Karen Loritts, author; conference speaker; blogger, *MomLife Today*; mother of four and grandmother of eight

"In this fine book on prayer you will find no super-spiritual hype nor dry detachment, but robust and sensitive exposition. Philip has put us all in his debt by this little book, which can be read with enjoyment in one sitting but will reward repeated study and will give both challenge and encouragement."

Bob Fyall, Senior Tutor, The Cornhill Training Course, Scotland

"I found my heart and will deeply moved by the key premise of this book: that we learn about prayer by learning about God. He speaks—are we listening to him? He sends his Son—are we responding to him? He is sovereign—do we trust him and think his thoughts after him? He sends his Spirit—do we realize we're empowered to pray? Internalize these great Bible truths, and your prayer life will come alive."

Rico Tice, evangelist; author, *Christianity Explored*

"It's refreshing not to have another Christian how-to book. Philip takes us right in by the front door and down the stairs to examine the very foundation of prayer. As he presses us to face the *why*, we also find help with the *what* and the *how*. I found these studies an essential exercise in thinking, a welcome source of relief, and a gentle lure to repentance."

Dale Ralph Davis, Professor Emeritus of Old Testament, Reformed Theological Seminary

Why We Pray

Why
We
Pray

WILLIAM PHILIP

ivp

INTER-VARSITY PRESS
Norton Street, Nottingham NG7 3HR, England
Email: ivp@ivpbooks.com
Website: www.ivpbooks.com

Published by Crossway, a publishing ministry of Good News Publishers,
Wheaton, Illinois 60187, USA.

This edition published by arrangement with Crossway. All rights reserved.

First published 2015

British Library Cataloguing in Publication Data
A catalogue record for this book is available from the British Library.

ISBN: 978–1–78359–196–1

Typeset in the United States of America
Printed and bound in Great Britain by Ashford Colour Press Ltd, Gosport,
Hampshire

*Inter-Varsity Press publishes Christian books that are true to the Bible and that
communicate the gospel, develop discipleship and strengthen the church for its
mission in the world.*

*Inter-Varsity Press is closely linked with the Universities and Colleges Christian
Fellowship, a student movement connecting Christian Unions in universities and
colleges throughout Great Britain, and a member movement of the International
Fellowship of Evangelical Students. Website: www.uccf.org.uk*

To the memory of my father, James Philip

His prayers, especially those from the
pulpit of Holyrood Abbey Church,
Edinburgh, were an enriching benediction
for which I and countless others will
give thanks all the days of our lives.

Contents

Foreword

In the pregnant pause between the ascension and Pentecost there is a prayer meeting in Jerusalem. Jesus had instructed his followers to wait for the promised Holy Spirit in order that they might take the gospel to the end of the earth. Luke records the gathering of the eleven apostles in the upper room. "All these with one accord were devoting themselves to prayer, together with the women and Mary the mother of Jesus, and his brothers" (Acts 1:14). It is no exaggeration to say that the church was born in prayer and that the subsequent growth of the Word and of the church cannot be explained apart from their prayers. Jesus had made it clear to them that apart from him they could do nothing (John 15:5), and he had also taught them that if they knew how to give good gifts to their children, to a far greater extent the Father would give good gifts to them that asked him (Matt. 7:11; Luke 11:13). Throughout Acts we find the church at prayer.

In seeking a replacement for Judas they prayed for guidance (Acts 1:24). When Peter and John were confronted by opposition and threats, they lifted their voices together to the sovereign Lord and prayed that they might continue to speak the Word with all boldness (Acts 4:29). When the practical demands of a growing church became the occasion of discord, the apostles made it clear that nothing must divert them from the priority of prayer and the ministry of the Word (Acts 6:4).

This thread of earnest, united, believing prayer is woven throughout the fabric of the early church. When Herod had killed James, and it looked as though Peter was next, "earnest prayer for him was made to God by the church" (Acts 12:5). The commissioning of Barnabas and Saul took place in the context of worship and prayer (Acts 13:3). As Derek Thomas observes, "The New Testament Church had grasped the essential truth that the God who ordains the end of all things has also ordained the means of its accomplishment."[1]

This should not surprise us because this pattern of prevailing prayer was one that the disciples had learned from spending time with the Lord Jesus. It becomes clear from reading the Gospels that prayer was established in Jesus's life as a holy habit. After an intense evening when Jesus healed the sick and dealt with the demons, the disciples searched for Jesus. He wasn't where they expected because, "rising very early in the morning, while it was still dark, he departed and went out to a desolate place, and there he prayed" (Mark 1:35). Similarly, before the selection of the twelve disciples, "he went out to the mountain to pray, and all night he continued in prayer to God" (Luke 6:12).

On the Mount of Olives, as he faced the grim reality of the crucifixion, "he withdrew from them about a stone's throw, and knelt down and prayed" (Luke 22:41). It is no wonder that on one such occasion one of the disciples asked him to teach them how to pray (Luke 11:1). Presumably the reality and intensity of his prayers caused those closest to him to want to learn the secret of real prayer. We might all be grateful for the man's request, for it is surely one with which we find ourselves identifying. In our Christian lives nothing is more important and nothing more difficult to maintain than a meaningful prayer life. Having warned against heaping up empty phrases (Matt. 6:7), Jesus provided his followers with a prayer that may be used as it stands. Although all the pronouns are plural and so fit worship that is corporate and public, the prayer may also be employed to our benefit in private. Although it is routinely referred to as the "Lord's Prayer," we might better think of it as the Disciple's Prayer in that he gave it to his followers to employ as they approach their heavenly Father.

The one hundredth question in the Westminster Shorter Catechism asks, "What does the preface of the Lord's Prayer teach us?" and provides the answer: "It teaches us to draw near to God with all holy reverence and confidence, as children to a father; able and ready to help us, and that

we should pray with and for others." Every time we re-
peat this prayer we are reminded that our fellowship with
God, through his son Jesus Christ, finds its principal expression in prayer. Our ability to call God "Father" is on
account of his grace. "In love he predestined us for adoption
as sons through Jesus Christ, according to the purpose of
his will, to the praise of his glorious grace, with which he
has blessed us in the Beloved" (Eph. 1:4–5). It is true that
God has a kind of fatherhood of all by creation, but this is
a prayer for those who are his by redemption, who have
received the spirit of sonship, enabling them to cry, "Abba,
Father." When we come to trust in Christ we receive the
right to become God's children. By grace we are welcomed
into a family to which we do not belong by nature. Martin
Luther referred to this prayer as "the greatest martyr on
earth," because it was used so frequently without thought
or feeling, without reverence or faith. In the pages that follow, Dr. Philip helps to ensure that this will not be true of
us, not just in terms of the Lord's Prayer, but also in every
expression of prayer. As one of the author's mentors help-
fully observed:

> Prayer for the Christian is a matter of believing that God
> is, and that he does respond to those who believe in
> him. Prayer then, instead of being a matter of times and
> seasons and special or routine occasions, becomes a life,
> or it becomes such a vital part of life that it re-focuses
> one's whole outlook. We become interested in God, his

ways, his doings, his words and we find ourselves agreeing with him about perhaps a great many things we were tempted not to agree about before. And the very humility which unself-consciously comes with such an attitude is one of sheer delight.

John Bunyan testified to such delight during the twelve years he spent in prison for unlawful preaching of the Bible. In communion with God he was enabled to write most of his literary and theological works, including in 1662, *A Discourse Touching Prayer*, in which he provides a wonderful definition of prayer:

Prayer is a sincere, sensible, affectionate pouring out of the heart or soul to God, through Christ, in the strength and assistance of the Holy Spirit, for such things as God has promised, or according to His Word, for the good of the church, with submission in faith to the will of God.

My earliest awareness of this kind of believing prayer was in hearing my parents pray for me when they thought I was already asleep. Along with that, I was always intrigued by the mats stored in one of the halls in our church building. When I enquired about them, I learned that they were used for kneeling during the Friday night prayer. It occurred to me that those adults must really believe that God answers prayer. Since then I have realized the various hindrances we meet when coming to God in prayer. Reminding myself of a number of useful observations has helped me:

If our prayer is meager, it is because we regard it as supplemental and not fundamental.

We can do more than pray after we have prayed but not until we have prayed.

We do not pray for the work. Prayer is the work and preaching is gathering up the results.

God does not delay to hear our prayers because he has no mind to give; but that by enlarging our desires, he may give us the more largely.

So then it is my prayer that the pages of this book will encourage each of us to "continue steadfastly in prayer, being watchful in it with thanksgiving" (Col. 4:2).

Alistair Begg
Parkside Church
Chagrin Falls, Ohio

Introduction

As a pastor, I had often felt I ought to preach a series on prayer. But I have to confess that I had always been put off doing so because so many of the sermons I have heard about prayer have made me feel rather depressed.

You know the kind of thing: somebody will tell you, with fervent emotion, about a great preacher getting up at four o'clock every morning and praying for six hours before breakfast, and if only you would do the same, it will be the secret to unlocking the spiritual blessing in your life. I'm afraid I just find that sort of thing really disheartening. I find I'm doing very well indeed if I can manage to pry myself out of bed at all before breakfast, never mind have hours of prayer. That kind of pious exhortation, which no doubt is genuinely intended to make me determined to go on praying and not give up, well, it just makes me want to give up altogether even before I've begun.

I may well simply be more perverse than you are, but that's the effect that kind of sermon has on me. It wouldn't surprise me to find that many Christians feel the same.

Some time ago, however, as I was thinking about how I could encourage my Christian brothers and sisters in prayer rather than discouraging and depressing them, I was reading a book that I found to be one of the most helpful I can recall ever reading on this subject. It was not a light book; it was a substantial biblical theology of prayer, with plenty to excite the neurons and tax the gray matter.[2] But the reason I found it so helpful was that in looking at what the whole Bible teaches about prayer, it reminded me of something very important: that we learn most about *prayer* simply by learning about *God*. That is a great thing to be reminded of, because the real truth about God is never discouraging. The Lord himself is never depressing as some very well-meaning and over-pious Christians often are, or can make you feel.

So after reading that book on prayer, which really turned out to be a book about knowing God, I found for the first time that I really did want to preach about prayer, because I thought I could prepare for it without getting depressed, and I could perhaps preach on it without depressing and discouraging others. (There can surely be no worse crime for any preacher than to depress and discourage the people of God.) I discovered that as I focused the congregation on God himself, asking the most basic question of all—Why do we pray?—we found immense encouragement in our relationship with the Lord and real help in the chief expression of that relationship, which is prayer.

As a church fellowship, made up of Christian people of

all ages and stages, as well as those still exploring the faith, we found these studies together to be a real blessing. They are offered here in the hope that others too may find the Bible's *explanation* of the nature of prayer, rather than mere *exhortation* about our need to pray, similarly liberating.

In the beginning, God created the heavens and the earth. The earth was without form and void, and darkness was over the face of the deep. And the Spirit of God was hovering over the face of the waters. And God said . . .

Genesis 1:1–3a

1

We Pray Because
God Is a Speaking God

The most important question to ask first about prayer is—
Why? Why do we pray? Not, Why *should* we pray? We
begin not with an exhortation but with an explanation:
why prayer exists at all, as it were. Why is there such a
thing as prayer? Prayer is speaking to God, but—just think
about it for a moment—why should there be any such thing
as speaking to God? Why would God want us to speak to
him? Why would God *need* us to speak to him if he controls all things, as he does? Why would we need to speak to
God just because he's there? We have a queen in the United
Kingdom, but I don't speak to the queen, and I don't suppose you do either—not very often, anyway. Why should
we speak to *God* just because he is a powerful being and our
sovereign ruler and Lord?

At its most basic and fundamental level, we pray because

God is a speaking God. Prayer derives from who and what God is, and the great feature of the God of the Bible, the God of the Christian faith, is that he is a speaking God. That is evident from the very first chapter of the Bible.

God Spoke the Whole Creation into Being

Creation begins with the voice of God, with God speaking: "And God said, 'Let there be light,' and there was light" (Gen. 1:3). And so it goes on. "And God said" is the refrain of the whole chapter. Then we come to these crucial words:

> Then God said, "Let us make man in our image, after our likeness. And let them have dominion over the fish of the sea and over the birds of the heavens and over the livestock and over all the earth and over every creeping thing that creeps on the earth."
>
> So God created man in his own image,
>   in the image of God he created him;
>   male and female he created them.
>   (Gen. 1:26–27)

Here is the first thing to think about: all the way through the opening chapter of the Bible, creation happens as God *speaks* the whole of the created order into being. He didn't just imagine it into existence, as no doubt he could have done. He didn't wave a magic wand and bring it out of his hat. According to Scripture he spoke it into being. "Let there be light," and light was. "Let there be creatures," and creatures were, including man. He spoke into existence everything we see.[3]

Now, why so? Well, because (and we'll think more about this presently) the creator God is, as the Bible tells us, the *covenant* God, which means he is not a distant deity; he is not aloof, disinterested, and far off but a God who is involved intimately and totally with everything he makes, from the sparrows that fall to the ground that Jesus tells us about (Matt. 10:29), to the very hairs of our heads, to the hills, to the valleys, to the rivers, to everything. God is a God of committed, covenant relationship.

When you think about it, this is what speech does; speech creates relationship. In fact, speech requires relationship. You can't speak to someone without creating a relationship. It might be a very short and cursory relationship, like the one you have with the bus driver when you get on and say, "Does this bus go to Buchanan Street?" and he says, "Yes—hop on!" You've created a relationship. It's rather shallow, but it's a relationship. At the other end of the spectrum are relationships that are lifelong and deep. I suppose the most obvious of those is marriage. But whatever the nature of the relationship, you can't create or sustain an ongoing relationship without speech (or at least some form of surrogate for the spoken word).

Genesis 1 tells us of a God who created the world in perfect relationship with himself and of a creation that, as it were, speaks back its praise to God its creator. God saw

23

everything he had made, we are told, and it was very good.
That was creation's speech back to God. The whole of the
created order was telling God, by everything in its very
nature, "This is very good!"

Many parts of the Bible echo this truth. Psalm 19 reminds us of it when it tells us, "The heavens declare the
glory of God, and the sky above proclaims his handiwork"
(v. 1). Psalm 96 calls on the whole of creation to speak forth
praise to God: "Let the heavens be glad, and let the earth
rejoice; let the sea roar, and all that fills it; let the field exult,
and everything in it!" (v. 11). Psalm 98, likewise, speaks of
the seas, the rivers, and the hills—of all creation—speaking
back to the God who spoke them into being. So you could
say that the whole of the created order, in a sense, prays;
it speaks back its praise to God the creator, to the one to
whom it owes everything, even its existence. Because God
spoke everything into being, he spoke all creation, therefore, into a relationship with himself.[4]

Of course, these verses also tell us about God's speaking humans into being. He did that as the crowning glory
of creation in a unique way. In Genesis 1:26 we find an
astonishing thing; we hear God speaking to himself: "Let
us make man," he says, "in our image." Don't you think
that is an extraordinary statement? The passage is recorded
by Moses, the great leader and teacher of Israel, the Moses
whose constant message was that Israel must be devoted
always and only to the *one* God. All through their wilder-

ness journeyings, and at Sinai, and in his final exhortations on the plains of Moab as Moses prepared Israel for their life in the land, he repeatedly emphasized that their God, the true God, is *one*. The Lord is not like the many gods and idols of the pagans who lived in the lands round about. He is the *one* God and the *only* God. Moses also teaches the famous Shema, the great prayer of the Israelite people: "Hear, O Israel: The LORD our God, the LORD is *one*" (Deut. 6:4). This is the very essence of the biblical faith: God is *one*, not many. Yet here in the first chapter of the Bible, we have the one God speaking to himself, using the *plural* terms "us" and "our": "Let us make man in our image."

Of course, we who have the fullness of the revelation of God through his ultimate word to us in Jesus Christ can understand this (at least, as far as it is possible for finite beings to understand the infinite God). We know that the one God is also three distinct persons: Father, Son, and Holy Spirit. We know God as the Holy Trinity, indivisible, inseparable; one God, but nevertheless, as the Scripture testifies, a God who speaks within himself and who is in perfect relationship with himself. So we should not be too surprised to see that perfect relationship in evidence here, way back at the dawn of creation, any more than we should be surprised that much later in history, John's Gospel records Jesus, the incarnate Son of God on earth, speaking in the Spirit to his heavenly Father. (Indeed, as part of that very prayer, in John 17:5, Jesus speaks explicitly of the glory he shared with the Father before the world existed.) The one God has always been, from all eternity, before all creation, the triune God, the relational, covenant God, the speaking God.

Here is the vital point for us in all this. According to the Bible, it is uniquely in the image of this God, this God of relationship, this speaking God, that we are made. "Let *us* make man in *our* image, after *our* likeness." And that is why, fundamentally, we human beings speak. That is why we human beings are relational, covenantal beings; it is because we image the relational, covenant, speaking God.

Just consider for a moment the way speech, communication, is intrinsic to our human nature. We can hardly imagine what it would be like to be denied any communication. That would be for us to become subhuman. In fact, we use that very language, such as when we talk about people who have lost all communicative capacity as being in a persistent vegetative state. They are totally unable to communicate with others. When we refer to people as being in a "vegetative state," we are saying that they are not really like human beings anymore. They are, tragically, more like vegetables.

We also know that to deny real relational interaction will ultimately dehumanize people. That's why sensory deprivation can be used so horribly in torture; when people are denied all communication, it unhinges them. You might remember years ago when the Eastern Bloc of Europe was for the first time exposed to the West after the fall of the Berlin Wall. Awful pictures appeared on our television screens of some of the orphanages in Romania where children had been abandoned and treated so horrifically. No one ever spoke to those babies and young children. There had been no speech, no communication, no warmth of human relationship, no belonging—none of these essential aspects that comprise normal humanity. As a result, not only their emotions but also their intellect and even their physical growth were stunted.

We human beings are made *as* human beings for *relationship*. By our nature, we are covenantal beings, because fundamental to our creation is the purpose that we should image the covenant, relational God. The most intimate reflection of this image in the created order is marriage. Marriage is a living illustration, in the flesh, of our relational nature, because in marriage two become one flesh. That is why to marriage, and to marriage alone, according to the Scriptures, belongs that deepest and most intimate relational communication, the physical, fleshly "speech" of sexual intercourse.

Above all, of course, we are spoken into being for a relationship not just with one another but with God himself. Man was created for that perfect, harmonious relationship with the God of creation *and* to be in perfect relationship with the whole of that creation over which God had placed human beings. Genesis 1:28 tells us, "God blessed them. And God said to them, 'Be fruitful and multiply and fill the earth and subdue it, and have dominion over . . . the earth.'"

There's not a hint there, as some have tried to claim, of exploitation of the earth; this verse is not the root of all the problems in ecology in our world today. Far from it. Pictured here is rather a perfectly ordered relationship between human beings and their world. It's a picture of man imaging God's gracious relationship over his creation, in his place, because it flows out of a perfect relationship between human beings and their God.

The whole of Genesis 1 and 2 paints a picture of that perfect relationship. God commands man as his vice-regent to rule over the earth. He sets him to work in the garden of Eden. Genesis 2:15 tells us that the Lord God took the man and put him in the garden to work it and keep it. By the way, the Hebrew word translated "put him" is literally "gave him rest." God gave him *rest* in the garden of Eden to work it and keep it. Perfect rest for man is doing the work of God. We should remember that. In fact, all the way through the Old Testament God lays before his people the promise of the future of *rest* in his land, and that is what God lays before us too; a glorious Sabbath rest still awaits the people of God (Heb. 4:9). Sometimes we think that when we go to heaven (or, more properly, when God's eternal kingdom fully comes), we're going to sit about doing nothing, but that's not true. The perfect rest of God is doing the work of God, and that is the eternal calling that awaits his people.

We see that glorious situation here, right in the beginning, in Genesis 1 and 2. God puts man in the garden, at perfect rest, in perfect harmony, to work under his direction. He speaks his gracious words of command to human beings, and the man and the woman respond obediently to God's direction. That's the visible form, if you like, of their trust in God, the *visible* form of expressing that right relationship with God, which they were created for. The New Testament calls it the obedience of faith (Rom. 1:5). But the *audible* form of that right relationship with God, of that trust, is their speech with God, their *verbal communion* with him. Apparently, God had the habit of taking an evening stroll in the garden of Eden to have a chat with Adam and Eve all about the goings-on of the day, because when we come to Genesis 3:9, God comes looking for them and asks, "Where are you?" He wanted to talk. The Lord God called to the man, "Where are you?"

That was the problem. God had spoken the whole creation into being and created man as a speaking being in his likeness so that above all he might enjoy relationship with man, calling out to him and receiving a joyful answer that would nurture ongoing fellowship and friendship. But something happened.

Man Stopped Answering God

Man stopped answering God. Adam hid. The Lord God called, "Where are you?" and Adam said, "I heard the sound of you in the garden, and I was afraid, because I was naked, and I hid myself" (Gen. 3:9). He hid because the human beings had cheated on that exclusive relationship with God, which they were created for. As we all know, when the communion of an exclusive relationship is broken, communication breaks down.

The newspaper columnists love to talk nowadays about the "special relationship" that Britain used to have with the United States. Remember Margaret Thatcher and Ronald Reagan? We were led to believe they were always on the phone together. If poor old Ronald Reagan stepped out of line, Maggie was on the phone putting him right, just like that. But they had, it seemed, a great relationship. It seemed to be similar with Tony Blair and George Bush, although they are very different characters. But it appears things are different now. Barack Obama and Gordon Brown didn't hit it off, and David Cameron has not fared a lot better, because all kinds of things have happened to put a strain on whatever had made the relationship special. The freeing of the Lockerbie bomber by the Scottish government dented transatlantic harmony, and the BP disaster in the Gulf of Mexico hardly helped. You certainly don't get the impression that the special red phone on the desk at 10 Downing Street is ringing nearly so often these days with a request from the incumbent of the White House for a congenial evening yarn. No special relationship, no communication.

Or think about a marriage. When a marriage is in trouble, what is the first sign? Husband and wife are not *talking* anymore. Perhaps first that deeper intimacy of sexual intercourse tails off and is gradually lost, but ultimately it is all kinds of communication. "We don't talk anymore!" as Cliff Richard put it. And when you don't talk, you live increasingly separate lives, because *speech is the audible form of a real and living relationship.* If there's no speaking happening, there's no relationship.

If you shout to somebody in the street, "Hello John!" and he doesn't answer but just continues walking, well, you know it's not John. He doesn't *know* you; that's why he doesn't answer. Recently I was walking down the street in the center of Glasgow, when I saw one of our students from the Cornhill Training Course, a girl with a long pigtail, on her bicycle at the traffic lights in front of me. I was just about to yank on her pigtail (since I've always thought that to be the purpose of pigtails), when the person on the bike turned around, and I saw it was somebody quite different; in fact it was a rather wild-looking man. It would have been very embarrassing to yank on the pigtail and discover an angry man thinking, "Who on earth are you?" Pigtail pulling just isn't a form of communication that can take place outside a good relationship with someone you know very well.

Meaningful speech, communication, and healthy relationship go together. Conversely, when communication is cut off completely, there can't be an ongoing relationship. Alas, that is where Genesis 3 leaves humanity:

Then the LORD God said, "Behold, the man has become like one of us in knowing good and evil. Now, lest he reach out his hand and take also of the tree of life and eat, and live forever"—therefore the LORD God sent him out from the garden of Eden to work the ground from which he was taken. He drove out the man, and at the east of the garden of Eden he placed the cherubim and a flaming sword that turned every way to guard the way to the tree of life. (vv. 22–24)

So, tragically, early in his story, man is shut out of the garden of God. He is shut out from hearing God's voice. He is barred from talking to God. There are no more strolls in the cool of the day. There is just total silence. Man has refused to respond to God's gracious words; he has taken his own way, and, therefore, with great sadness, God has to say, "Okay, you won't listen. I'll stop the conversation. I'll back off." So man, created as human for communion with God, became, well, subhuman, not talking anymore to God, who made him. That's pretty much the way the world has been ever since. Man won't listen to God; he puts his fingers in his ears and says, "I don't need to listen to this! I reject God, if there is a God. I don't need God. I'll live as my own God. I'm not listening." It's a bit like a cross teenager who storms into the bedroom, slams the door, and turns up the music so that he can't hear his parents' voices if they're calling him, and he hopes because the music is so awful his parents will stay away.

Anyone with teenage children knows all about that, just as they also know that such behavior doesn't, in fact, solve teenage angst. Hiding away and refusing to listen to reason doesn't bring happiness and peace and fulfillment. Nor has it done so for our world or the lives of the people of our world, and that is the tragedy of the human condition. That's why we are as we are, and that's why the world is as it is. God created us for speech, for communion, for relationship with him, and yet we have broken that relationship because we have refused to respond. As a result, we can't relate to God, even if we want to. We don't talk anymore, and we can't talk anymore. There's nothing to say. Our relationship is in irretrievable breakdown.

But God Would Not Stop Speaking to Man

The Bible is plain about both the cause and the consequences of this catastrophe (read, for example, Rom. 1:18–2:5). Yet it tells us equally plainly something more, something barely believable but deeply wonderful. It tells us that despite all this, the God of the Bible has not stopped speaking to us.

We know that when a relationship is destroyed by unfaithfulness, it is impossible for the guilty party simply to reinitiate that relationship. The guilty one doesn't have the power or the right to do that. Far too much has been forfeited, so much that a huge price must be paid before reconciliation can happen, the immeasurably costly price of forgiveness. The truth is that only the wronged party is in a position to invite the guilty party back in. That's because the wronged party alone must bear the cost of that forgiveness. It's desperately costly to forgive, to be able to say to one's abuser, "Yes, you can come back into this relationship."

We see that all the time in the news these days, sadly, with our sporting stars, the top golfers and football players and their infidelities. Only if the wronged party—in these notorious cases, the men's wives—condescends to initiate that communication is there any possibility whatsoever of the relationship being repaired and coming back into being in any real and meaningful way. No matter how rich you are, when you are the unfaithful one who has messed it all up, all you can do is respond; you cannot initiate anything. All you have power to say is, "Yes, please, I do want back into this marriage," and you can only say that *in answer to an invitation from the person whom you've wronged.*

So it is with God.

But the whole story of the Bible, the whole story of the gospel, is of a God who, from the very beginning, determined that he would say those words, "I want you to come back in. Yes, the rift is terrible; yes, the pain has been absolutely unspeakable; yes, the cost to me will be infinite. *But I will bear that cost* so that once again you will be truly human, creatures made for me, to be with me, to know me, to be able to converse with me and commune with me intimately, so that you will be able to answer me again, and we shall be able to talk together as friends."

That is what God did. He called out in grace to human beings on the basis of a great promise: "Yes, one day I *will* deal forever with all the pain, vast disappointment, and righteous anger in my heart brought about by what you have done. *I* will deal with that; *I* will bear the cost because I *want* you to know me again. I *want* you to hear my voice. I *want* you to rejoice in speaking to me again and coming to tell me all the things you want to tell me, to have that relationship of a son with a father once again."

So it was. God called out to Abraham, to Isaac, to Jacob, and to countless others after them, and they were able to answer him. They spoke to each other. Exodus 33:11 tells us that God spoke to Moses face-to-face, just as a man speaks to his friend. All these spoke with God because they knew God again. They had a real relationship with God because they had responded to his call, to his voice calling out to trust him, to believe in him, to obey him. In other words, they had what the Bible calls "faith."

How do we know Abraham had faith? Well, Hebrews 11:8 is plain. We know he had faith because he obeyed God when God called him. When God spoke to him and told him to go out to a place that he never knew, he responded and obeyed: "By faith Abraham obeyed when he was called." We might say that Abraham's obedience was the *visible* form of his faith. But the *audible* form of his faith, of his real and living relationship with God, was that he talked with God. God spoke to Abraham that word of great promise, and Abraham responded. "Abraham called upon the name of the LORD" (Gen. 12:8). In other words, *Abraham prayed.*

Prayer was the audible form of Abraham's faith, as it is of all faith. Speaking to God in prayer is simply the audible response to God's call to us, just as following him in obedience is the visible response to the call that marks out real faith and is the evidence of a real and living knowledge of God. Prayer is responding to God's gracious word of salvation in his wonderful promise of his saving gospel. And if Hebrews 1 tells us that God spoke his ultimate word in the person of his Son, the Lord Jesus Christ, then that means fundamentally that prayer is simply *responding in faith to the Lord Jesus Christ*.

Prayer is answering God's call to human beings in Jesus, answering it with all that we are and all that we have, not just with our lips but with our lives, so that our words, in that sense, are simply vocalizing what's on the inside. It's the inside reality coming out in an audible form. I remember my father explaining it to me this way: "It's not so much *what* we pray but *what we are* when we pray that matters." That's true, because real prayer is anything that comes from a heart truly responding to the Lord Jesus Christ. It is the multitude of responses that come from a life that has found Christ.

In Acts 9, when we read of the conversion of Saul of Tarsus, the Lord tells Ananias where to find Saul and says, "Behold, he is praying" (v. 11). Why is that so significant? Saul of Tarsus had said his prayers all the days of his life as a pious Pharisee. But for all his prayers, he had never really prayed before, because as yet he had never truly answered God's call. But when he met God personally, in Jesus Christ the risen Lord, he truly prayed. He communicated with God.

You can't respond until God has called out to you to respond. You can't say, "I do," until somebody has asked, "Will you marry me?" But in Jesus, God has broken that heavenly silence. He has called out. He has said, "I *do* want you back. Will you *have* me?" And he wants you to say yes. Saying yes to that call of Jesus is the essence, and the beginning, of all real prayer.

So let me ask you this: Are you a praying person?

I'm not asking whether you *say* your prayers—anybody can fool himself into thinking he's praying because he's saying his prayers. But are you a praying person? Are you responding from the very bottom of your heart to the Lord Jesus Christ, to God's call to you in the gospel of Christ? Are you answering audibly and visibly the God who has called out to you in Jesus his Son? Are you doing *that*?

If you are doing that, you are praying.

But until you do that, well, you can say all the prayers you like, but you have never really prayed at all. Because praying is answering that wonderful call of God.

It's never too late to start really praying, and you *can* pray, because *God is a speaking God*. He has called out to us, wonderfully, in the message of his Son, the Lord Jesus. He wants us to be answering people.

Questions for Reflection or Discussion

1. In the foreword Alistair Begg wrote, "In our Christian lives nothing is more important and nothing more difficult to maintain than a meaningful prayer life." Have you found this to be true in your life? In what ways is prayer difficult for you? What are the obstacles to maintaining a vibrant prayer life?

2. We learn most about prayer simply by learning about God. What truths have you learned about God that have impacted your prayer life? What spiritual disciplines do you practice that help your prayer life?

3. How does the fact that God is a covenant God impact your prayer life? Is this idea new to you, and if so, how do you hope it will change your prayer life?

4. Whatever the nature of the relationship, you can't create, or sustain, an ongoing relationship without speech (or at least some form of surrogate for the spoken word). What types of communication might be substituted for full-fledged words? How might this play out in person-to-person communication when someone lacks the capacity for true speech? What are the implications of these ideas for our prayers during times of extreme emotional stress or deep sorrow, when words don't come easily?

5. Philip differentiates between visible relationship (obedience) and audible relationship (words). What does it look like

to have visible relationship without verbal communion, and what are the effects of having one but not the other? Is it possible to truly have one without the other when it comes to humans relating to God?

6. The chapter concludes that "prayer is simply responding in faith to the Lord Jesus Christ." How have you found this to be true in your own life? If you truly believed and lived out the truth that we pray because God is a speaking God, what would change about your prayer life? Given this definition of prayer, are you a praying person? Or do you just say prayers without truly relating to God?

Now when all the people were baptized, and when Jesus also had been baptized and was praying, the heavens were opened, and the Holy Spirit descended on him in bodily form, like a dove; and a voice came from heaven, "You are *my beloved Son*; with you I am well pleased."

Luke 3:21–22

2

We Pray Because
We Are Sons of God

It's easy for a preacher to repeatedly exhort people to pray, but the trouble is that this usually just makes people feel guilty without making them any more likely to pray. Our concern in this book, by contrast, is not with an exhortation to pray but with an explanation of prayer.

We have seen that at the most basic, we pray because God himself is a speaking God. We pray because of who and what God is. God speaks, and we answer him; we were created to respond to him. That's what our existence is all about. God spoke the whole of creation into being, and all of creation answers back to God. But he made human beings in his likeness, above all other creatures in creation, to enjoy an intimate, special relationship, a relationship of love that shares in the life of God himself. Absurdly, irrationally, and disastrously, we rebelled against God, destroying that relationship. So everything fell silent. There was no more answering God. Mankind was banished from the fellowship with God that he had hitherto known and enjoyed. There was no more prayer, no talk, no sweet communion between God and human beings. Only silence. Thus the first book of C. S. Lewis's Space Trilogy is called *Out of the Silent Planet*.[5] In it Lewis portrays earth as a planet exiled from the rest of the solar system, and people from all the other worlds refer to it as the "silent planet" because, of all of those worlds, earth is the one that has no communication with what he calls "deep heaven," the place where God himself dwells. The silent planet—the end of intimate communication with God, the end of prayer.

We have also seen that the story of the gospel is the restoration of true prayer; it is the story of the restoration of real relationship between man and God. Down through the ages God has called out to man, and his last and ultimate word and call to human beings has been in the person of his only Son. Jesus Christ is God's ultimate word to man. So the very essence of real prayer is simply answering God in the call that comes to us in Jesus Christ. Prayer is responding to Jesus. We can pray because God is a speaking God, because we have been *created* to respond to him, and because through Jesus Christ we have been *redeemed* that we might again respond to him.

We need to take things a bit further as we consider the centrality of the person of our Lord Jesus Christ in our discussion of prayer. It's not just that God calls out to us ultimately in Jesus Christ his Son; it's that we can respond to God only through Jesus Christ. Jesus is not only God's ultimate word to man but also man's ultimate word of response to God. It is only in Jesus, and in his relationship with the Father, that the perfect relationship of humanity is fully restored to all its glory, to its intimate fellowship with God, our heavenly Father.

Jesus Is the True Son of God

The first thing we need to understand is that Jesus is the true Son of God. You might think that's obvious—we know Jesus is God's Son. But he is the *only* Son of God in the sense that he is the only *true human being*, and therefore he is the only *true pray-er* to God the world has seen since man's first rebellion at the beginning. Adam, remember, was created to be the son of God. That is the point being made in the genealogy in Luke, where Luke traces Jesus's origin back to Adam, "the son of God." Adam was made for a son's close relationship with God his father; he was to love and trust God and to rest in God's grace as his obedient son.

That was manifested in Adam's *life* before the fall (he was obedient to God's commands), and it was manifested just as much on his *lips*, that is, in his conversation with God, his prayer. Prayer was the audible evidence of that real relationship of obedient perfection between God and man. Prayer as deep and personal communion with God was uniquely the privilege of God's holy and obedient son Adam. God didn't go walking in the garden with a hippopotamus; he didn't call out to the armadillo or to the birds or to anything else—he called out to man.

But, as we noted earlier, Adam lost that status as God's holy son through his disobedience. We refer to the "fall" of man, but the Bible is much more specific. There is no sense in which that fall was something of an accident. It wasn't bad luck, like going out and falling on the ice; it wasn't that kind of fall at all. It was willful, deliberate disobedience. That's the language the apostle Paul uses when he speaks about it in Romans 5. It was one man's trespass, one man's disobedience that brought sin and condemnation and death to all men.[6] So it is perhaps more accurate to talk about the transgression of man, the breaking of the covenant God had made with man (see v. 14).[7]

However, in the coming of Jesus, the world has once again seen God's holy Son, another Adam—as the New Testament calls him, "the second man" (1 Cor. 15:47). What was it that the angel said to Mary about the child who would be born to her? "The child to be born" he said, "will be called holy—the Son of God" (Luke 1:35). In the Old Testament, God called his people Israel his "firstborn son" (Ex. 4:22). But Israel as the son of God was a constant failure. God also called the anointed kings of his people his special sons—above all, Solomon, the son of David: "He shall be to me a son," said the Lord (2 Sam. 7:14). Yet even

Solomon, after the brief moment of glory in the high point of his kingdom, fell away into sin and shame.[8] At last in Jesus of Nazareth is a true Son, a true human being, as God meant human beings to be, obedient in every aspect of his life. That perfect relationship of father and son was *visible* in his obedient life but also *audible* on his lips in the constant two-way communication between Jesus and his heavenly Father.

Not only did Jesus pray constantly to his Father in heaven but also his Father in heaven answered him. Heaven was never silent to the prayers of this man. There were no mediators needed, no priests to specially intercede between Jesus and his heavenly Father. This man had direct access to the Father because he was everything that Adam had failed to be, everything that Adam had rebelled against. He was the true Son of God in whom God was not disappointed and by whom God was not let down. As Luke relates, he is the Son in whom God delights, in whom he is well pleased. At his baptism God's voice spoke directly from the glory of heaven: "You are *my beloved Son*; with you I am well pleased" (Luke 3:22). Then immediately Luke explains exactly what that means as he unfolds the genealogy that goes all the way back to David, to Abraham, to Adam "the son of God" (Luke 3:38). Luke is telling us that Jesus is not only the true king of Israel, not only the true heir of all God's promises to Abraham, but that, at last, he is the true Adam. He is the true human being; he is the true Son of God. Then immediately Luke further demonstrates this for us in the account of Jesus's temptation in the wilderness:

> And Jesus, full of the Holy Spirit, returned from the Jordan and was led by the Spirit in the wilderness for forty days, being tempted by the devil. And he ate nothing during those days. And when they were ended, he was hungry. The devil said to him, "*If you are the Son of God*, command this stone to become bread." And Jesus answered him, "It is written, 'Man shall not live by bread alone.'" And the devil took him up and showed him all the kingdoms of the world in a moment of time, and said to him, "To you I will give all this authority and their glory, for it has been delivered to me, and I give it to whom I will. If you, then, will worship me, it will all be yours." And Jesus answered him, "It is written,
>
> > 'You shall worship the Lord your God,
> > and him only shall you serve.'"
>
> And he took him to Jerusalem and set him on the pinnacle of the temple and said to him, "*If you are the Son of God*, throw yourself down from here, for it is written,
>
> > 'He will command his angels concerning you,
> > to guard you,'
>
> and
>
> > 'On their hands they will bear you up,
> > lest you strike your foot against a stone.'"

And Jesus answered him, "It is said, 'You shall not put the Lord your God to the test.'" And when the devil had ended every temptation, he departed from him until an opportune time.

And Jesus returned in the power of the Spirit to Galilee, and a report about him went out through all the surrounding country. (Luke 4:1–14)

Like Adam at the beginning, Jesus, as the second man, the new Adam, was tempted by the Devil. He was tempted in exactly the same way to disobey God and to seek great things for himself. But where Adam failed, dreadfully, despite being surrounded by all the glory and perfection of Eden (surely the most perfect circumstances for obedience), Jesus triumphed. Jesus remained faithful, despite *his* testing being in the wilderness (not in a beautiful garden), amidst hunger (not in a place of plenteous food), and among the wild beasts (not the subservient animals of the garden). The environment in which Jesus plumbed the depth of his temptation was the very opposite of Eden. Yet he triumphed. Twice Satan taunted him. "If you are the Son of God," he says, "worship me and I'll give you all your heart's desire" (see vv. 3, 9). It's exactly what "that ancient serpent, who is the devil" (Rev. 20:2) said to Adam and Eve. But, no, said Jesus, for "it is written, 'You shall worship the Lord your God, and him only shall you serve'" (Luke 4:8).

Jesus was the true Son of God; he obeyed God his Father with the obedience of true faith. That's why we read in verse 14 that he returned to Galilee in the power of the Holy Spirit. His life was marked by constant communication with the Father, in the Spirit—that is, by constant, real prayer. That's why Jesus could stand at Lazarus's tomb and pray, "Father, I thank you that you have heard me. I knew that you always hear me" (John 11:41–42). He had no doubt whatsoever that God would hear and answer his prayer, just as in John 17, in the great prayer in the upper room, he made requests of his heavenly Father with absolute confidence, without a shadow of a doubt. All Jesus's prayers on earth were heard because he is the true Son of God, because he is the true and holy *man* as man was meant to be, communing intimately and constantly with the Father.

His prayers on earth were heard because of his "reverent submission" (Heb. 5:7 NIV). Moreover, Hebrews tells us that his prayers in heaven are heard for his people because he lives forever to make intercession for them (7:25). It's because he is the Son who has been made perfect forever (vv. 24, 28).[9] Jesus is the triumphant, holy Son of God. He is the last Adam, the second man, the new man. He is the true human being, and therefore his prayers are always heard. His prayers will always be acceptable to the Father. They will never be rebuffed, because he is God's holy Son, and he has infinite and unlimited access to him.

The story is told that one day President John F. Kennedy was in the Oval Office in a meeting with VIPs and leaders. Strict instructions had been given to White House staff and security that under no circumstances was anybody to come in and disturb this meeting. But at a crucial point in the tense talks and negotiations, suddenly the door flew open. Everybody looked startled; who would dare to defy the presidential decree? In marched a little boy. He walked straight up to the president, jumped up onto his knee, and cuddled in the lap of the most powerful man on earth. It was John F. Kennedy Jr., the son of the president. What no one else could have done, he was able to do without a moment's hesitation. He had privileged access, and no one could stop *him* from coming to see his father.

"Well, that's all very interesting," you might be saying to yourself, "but I can't quite understand what all this has got to do with me. What has all this theological talk about Jesus got to do with *my* prayer life? Tell me something practical."

In fact, the truth is that all practical help in the Christian life stems from theology, which literally means "words about God," because all useful learning about ourselves stems from learning about God. You may be thinking, *I can't see the relevance to my life of Jesus's being the true Son of God with unlimited access to the Father. I'm not Jesus! I can't pray as Jesus can. How does that help me? Where do I fit into this?*

Well, the answer that all this talk about Jesus (this theology) gives is that it's very relevant. The truth is, you *can* pray just like Jesus. You have the very same access to the Father that he has—if, that is, you are a Christian believer.

Through Jesus We Are True Sons of God

Through the gospel we also are made sons of God through Jesus Christ, which is the second vital thing we need to grasp. It's fundamental to all our praying. Prayer is the privilege that belongs only to God's beloved and holy Son. It is an address of intimacy; it is access to the God whose throne really does rule the whole world (not the president of the United States). Ours is a far greater access than that of the son of the president. Equally, if prayer is the privileged access of intimate relationship, then unless there is a real relationship of a son with a father, prayer just can't happen. Unless the relationship is real, prayer is just pretend.

There are only two people in this world who can call me "Dad." Actually, more often these days it's "Da-aaadd!" As all fathers recognize, there is a lovely but all too brief period when your little ones call you "Daddy"; then, before you know it, you have entered the stage where it's only "Da-aaad!"—the despairing, exasperated intonation of the teenager to whom you are but an embarrassing encumbrance. I'm well into that stage now, from which someone cheerily told me recently you never actually emerge (except perhaps for brief interludes when money or something else is being solicited, and then the cheerful salutation "Daddy" reappears). Regardless of the tone of voice, there are only two people who can call me Dad: my daughters. If somebody I didn't know shouted out "Dad!" I would assume she was not talking to me but to somebody else. Only my true children can call me Dad—father—unless, of course, others were to become my true children through adoption.

That is exactly what the gospel tells us God has done to those who have become united to Jesus through his great redemption. This is the extraordinary truth the apostle Paul teaches:

> In the same way we also, when we were children, were enslaved to the elementary principles of the world. But when the fullness of time had come, God sent forth his Son, born of woman, born under the law, to redeem those who were under the law, so that we might receive adoption as sons. And because you are sons, God has sent the Spirit of his Son into our hearts, crying, "Abba! Father!" So you are no longer a slave, but a son, and if a son, then an heir through God. (Gal. 4:3–7)

Adoption is the legal transfer of sonship from one father to another. Once, says the apostle, we were children in slavery to the world, or, as he puts it even more graphically in Ephesians 2:2, "sons of disobedience," following the prince of the power of the air, that is, the Devil. Strong language, isn't it? But it is the language Jesus uses; those who do not belong to him are sons of their father the Devil (John 8:44). Once you were that, says Paul, but now you have received "adoption as sons." Whose sons? God's sons. God sent his Son, Jesus, that we might receive all the status of Jesus and therefore all the privileges that are his and, above all, that marvelous privilege of intimate access to our heavenly Father in real prayer. Look at Galatians 4:6: "And because you are sons, God has sent the Spirit of his Son into our hearts, crying, 'Abba! Father!'"—the Spirit that guarantees us access, not to the office of the president, but to the office of the creator and ruler and judge of the whole universe.

We are all sons of God through faith (Gal. 3:26)—not just children but sons and full heirs. (Gender is not at issue here, but status; hence the insistence that we are sons, not just children. The point is that we all share in the full inheritance of the firstborn, Jesus himself.[10]) All who are baptized into Christ have "put on Christ" (v. 27). They have assumed Christ's personal clothing, that is, his status of sonship. It doesn't matter whether we're male or female; we are united to Jesus, *the* Son of God, which means everything that is his by right of birth is now ours by right of adoption. That's why we pray. In Jesus Christ we are all sons of God; we have received adoption, and now we all share the extraordinary, privileged, legal status before God the Father of Jesus himself, his only Son.

Now, this is of vital importance to grasp. Your prayers and mine will not be heard by God because of our *sincerity* but because of our *status*. We are sons of God, which means that God cannot *not* hear us. We are his sons. That's gospel truth. He can't not hear your prayers if you are in Christ. If we don't feel that at times, if it doesn't feel like it's true, it's simply because we are disbelieving the gospel that teaches it plainly to us. We are disbelieving our status as justified before God. We are disbelieving the reality of the legal status of adoption that is ours through faith in Jesus Christ. It really *is* ours; it has changed everything.

Concerning this image of adoption, I always tend to think of the wonderful, old film *Ben-Hur*, starring Charlton Heston. Perhaps, like me, you grew up thinking that a lot of Bible heroes looked like Charlton Heston, since he seemed to play most of them on the silver screen, such as Moses in Cecil B. DeMille's *The Ten Commandments*. I think I probably thought for a while that Ben-Hur is in the Bible, because he too was played by Charlton Heston. Anyway, in that film (if you haven't seen it, you must) Judah Ben-Hur is a rebellious Hebrew who becomes a slave in the galleys of Rome. After a shipwreck, he saves the master of the ship, a Roman lord, and in gratitude he adopts Ben-Hur to be his son. So the whole world changes: one who was once a slave on the galleys of Rome is now wearing the clothing of Rome, the splendid toga, and the ring and the seal of his father's house. At first he just can't believe the enormous change that has taken place. But the seal on his finger—the ring that stamps the authority of his new name and family, his new privilege and honor—reminds him it's true. He has become a real Roman with all the privileges of a real Roman.

That is the way it is with the Christian. We can pray, and God *will* hear us—not on the basis of our performance but on the basis of our privilege as sons adopted into the family of God. Therefore, being confident in prayer is not presumption; it is faith. It is simply honoring the Lord Jesus Christ and his great salvation, which God has given to us in his abundant mercy.

You may feel that you can't pray because you are unworthy, because you know you've sinned, because you've done things that you're ashamed of. But if you believe that your sin means you can't pray to your heavenly Father, then you have to realize that such thinking adds to your sin a terrible insult to the Lord Jesus Christ and everything he has done for you. If you say, "I can't pray to God because I'm so messed up," then what you are really saying is, "Jesus, you haven't done enough through your death on the cross to make me acceptable to God forever. You haven't done enough for God to really hear *my* prayers."

That's a blasphemous thing to say, and it treats the cross of Christ as though it was nothing, as though it was insufficient to justify your sin. But isn't that exactly what we are guilty of doing so often? We frequently base our assurance of acceptance before God, and therefore our standing with God, on our performance: "Have I really been good and faithful this week? Have I managed to resist sin? Have I done all the things I wanted to do to glorify God?" If you feel, "Well, yes, I've had quite a good week so maybe God will hear my prayers today and answer me," that's what gets you revved up to pray.

Or maybe you think, *If I pray long, intense, serious prayers, God will surely hear me. I'll be a real prayer warrior.*

Maybe I'll have a whole day set aside for prayer and fasting, or a whole night of prayer, or something like that. Maybe if I do all these things, then God will hear me. Friends, that is to disbelieve the gospel; it is to deny the gospel.

Jesus says that's paganism, not piety. In Matthew 6 Jesus says that we're not to pray long and intense prayers, heaping up phrases. That's what the pagans do. They think they'll be heard for their many words, for their impressive oratory. But they're all wrong, totally wrong! It's much simpler than that, he says, for those privileged to be the adopted sons of God. He tells us to pray to our Father in heaven, just giving thanks and laying out our needs, and God will hear us.

God *will* hear you. Because you are his son, he can't not hear you. You have put on Christ, you have come to the Father clothed in the righteousness of Jesus. His very own Spirit is in you, crying out along with your words, "Abba! Father!" When he hears you, he hears the voice of his Son. He really and truly is your Father. To doubt that, to act as though it isn't true, is to deny the very truth of the gospel itself. Your prayers and mine will not be heard because of *our* faithfulness but on account of Jesus's great faithfulness. Our prayers will be heard not because we deserve a hearing but because he does. Our prayers will be heard not because of our perfection but because of *his* marvelous perfection.

Therefore, we need to let the fact of Jesus and his sonship and our wonderful sharing in that extraordinarily privileged status fill all our thoughts about prayer—especially when doubts assail us. So often when we pray, we doubt. We think to ourselves, *Will God really hear my prayers? How could he really hear me? I'm so feeble*, or *I'm so sinful*, or *I'm so unsanctified*, or *I'm so un-prayer-warrior-like. Maybe God won't listen to me.*

But the gospel says no! It steers us away from ourselves and whether we're good or faithful enough. Don't go on at yourself saying things like, "Oh, I know I ought to pray more. I really must try." The truth is that all of us need to pray more, but if we start focusing on that, we'll lose our confidence in prayer. Don't think about yourself when you're thinking about prayer; think about the Lord Jesus Christ. Think about how faithful *he* is—always, always, always—for you. Think about how consistent he was in his visible faith, in his obedience to his heavenly Father. Think about how consistent he was in his audible faith, in his prayer to his heavenly Father. He was consistent in his life on earth for your sake, and, says the gospel, he is consistent in his intercession in heaven now for your sake. He is a priest forever, making intercession for you and me. Remember that you have put on Christ. Remember that you have received adoption as his son. Remember that his Spirit cries out, from your very own heart, the words you pray, saying, "Abba! Father!" How can that not be heard? It must be heard.

The truth of the gospel means that you can say, and I can say, and we *must* say just what Jesus said: "Father, I [know] that you always hear me" (John 11:41–42). We pray because in Jesus *we are sons of God*. We don't need to pray, and we mustn't pray, like those who don't know the Father, like those who lobby loud and long and do everything they can to try to win an audience with the president. No, we walk straight into the room. We mustn't pray like the pagans— full of impressive rituals and length and words and all of these things—in the hopes of impressing God into listening. No! We who know that we are sons through our Lord Jesus Christ can come confidently. We can come intimately. We can come always to our loving heavenly Father because that's what he is to us, through Jesus, forever.

Some years ago one of my daughters was badgering me to do something for her, and I pretended to be unwilling, saying, "Well, now, why should I do that for you? You need to give a really good reason to get me to stop reading my paper and come and help you." She got a bit frustrated trying to find a reasoned argument to convince me. She quickly ran out of ideas, and at last simply said, "Well, you have to because . . . because . . . because . . . *because you're my dad!*" The strange thing was that once she said that, well, how could I possibly resist my little girl?

That's the way it is with our heavenly Father. Through our union with Jesus, he can't not hear us. It doesn't matter what we've done. It doesn't matter what we've not done. We pray because we are sons of God.

Listen to what the Lord Jesus Christ, our elder brother,

tells us about his Father and our Father in the matter of our prayers:

> I tell you, ask, and it will be given to you; seek, and you will find; knock, and it will be opened to you. For everyone who asks receives, and the one who seeks finds, and to the one who knocks it will be opened. What father among you, if his son asks for a fish, will instead of a fish give him a serpent; or if he asks for an egg, will give him a scorpion? If you then, who are evil, know how to give good gifts to your children, how much more will the heavenly Father give the Holy Spirit to those who ask him! (Luke 11:9–13)

That's our heavenly Father, and we pray because we are sons of this God.

Questions for Reflection or Discussion

1. What misconceptions do people have about prayer—both believers and nonbelievers? What wrong ideas do you sometimes have about prayer, in practice if not in belief?

2. What is the fundamental truth about believers' standing before God that makes prayer possible and expected? How can you be sure that God will hear your prayers?

3. Most of us have prayer lives that ebb and flow—times when we feel close to God and pray frequently, and times when our prayers seem to hit the ceiling and go no further. What cir-

cumstances have led to times of deep communion with God? What circumstances have led to times when your prayer life feels dry? What conclusions can you draw about the practice of prayer from your answers to these questions?

4. Look back through the chapter at the Bible passages that portray Jesus's prayer life. What can we learn from his example in these passages, or in others that you are familiar with? What does studying the life of Christ teach us about how to pray?

5. Sometimes we put off praying because we feel unworthy or want to get our spiritual lives back on track first. Why is it blasphemous to say that you are too sinful to pray, or that you need to do x-y-z before you can approach God? In what ways does your practice of prayer diminish Christ's finished work on the cross?

6. Philip writes, "Don't think about yourself when you're thinking about prayer; think about the Lord Jesus Christ. Think about how faithful he is—always, always, always—for you." What starts to happen to your prayer life when you think about yourself too much? What happens to your prayer life when you think only about Jesus?

"Why did the Gentiles rage,
   and the peoples plot in vain?
The kings of the earth set themselves,
   and the rulers were gathered together,
against the Lord and against his Anointed"—

for truly in this city there were gathered together against your holy servant Jesus, whom you anointed, both Herod and Pontius Pilate, along with the Gentiles and the peoples of Israel, to do whatever your hand and your plan had predestined to take place.

Acts 4:25–28

3

We Pray Because
God Is a Sovereign God

Approaching the subject of prayer from the perspective of explanation—what prayer actually is, why prayer exists, and why it is possible at all—is much more encouraging than merely hearing exhortations to pray, because instead of focusing on ourselves, we focus on God. Thinking about what God does and who God is, is always far more encouraging than thinking about ourselves, about what we aren't, about what we don't do and what we should do more of.

So far, we have seen that we pray, fundamentally, because God is a speaking God. God calls out to us, and we answer. Despite our rebellion and infidelity, God did not keep silent. He called out to us supremely in the person of the Lord Jesus Christ, and we answer him audibly by faith. We pray. We call God our heavenly Father only because we have been adopted into his family; we have become sons of

God through the Spirit of Jesus Christ in our hearts, and we share that unique privilege of access at any time to the Father's presence. Like the son of the president, we too, as sons of Almighty God, can enter unhindered, as it were, into the Oval Office of heaven to be heard, no matter how many "Do not disturb" signs there might seem to be on the door. We pray because we are sons of God in Jesus Christ.

A third reason we pray explains why our prayers can be meaningful and effective and purposeful in both time and eternity: we pray *because God is a sovereign God.*

The Logic of God's Sovereignty

The logic of God's sovereignty—at first you might think that doesn't sound right, because it often seems to people that God's sovereignty is actually a problem for prayer, not a reason for prayer. Christians often say things like, "Well, look, if God is really sovereign, if he knows all things, and if he's predestined everything, then why should we pray at all? What's the point of praying if God decides and controls absolutely everything? I can't see the point of praying to a sovereign God."

Well, let me just turn that around for a moment and put the matter another way. What would be the point of praying, of asking God to do things and make things happen, if he *didn't* decide and control all things, and if he *wasn't* absolutely sovereign over every power and authority in this universe and every other? What would be the point of praying if God *couldn't* do the things we ask? If that were the case, then there really wouldn't be any point at all, would there? Prayer to a God who wasn't truly sovereign would indeed be a pointless exercise.

There is no point in lobbying the gardener at 10 Downing Street for a change in the law. He doesn't have any influence. Nobody donates money to be able to sit next to that gardener at a special dinner. But people do expend a lot of energy to get access to the occupant of "Number 10," the prime minister, and his government, precisely because in governing the nation, along with his cabinet ministers, he has sovereign power and authority to do things. Everyone knows that, which is why people want access to him. So it is with God.

The early church knew that perfectly well, which is why they prayed as they did in Acts 4. They were faced with the united opposition of all worldly powers, but they prayed to a sovereign God. Acts 4:24 tells us, "They lifted their voices together to God and said, 'Sovereign Lord . . . ,'" which means he is the God who "made the heaven and the earth and the sea and everything in them" and the God who spoke through the prophets long ago about exactly what was going to happen in the future, including the words of the psalmist David quoted here in Acts. The Bible reports, as the most natural thing in the world, the church offering urgent prayer petitions to a wholly sovereign God, who will nonetheless do "whatever your hand and your plan . . . predestined to take place" (v. 28).

Yet we do face what we see as a problem, because here, as in many other areas that pertain to our faith, the Bible can seem illogical.[11] It seems unreasonable that if God is truly sovereign, then we can be held wholly accountable, wholly responsible for our actions. If we are truly and utterly responsible, then how can God really be wholly and completely sovereign? It seems illogical. Well, it is a problem of logic. But the Bible tells us that it's a problem of our logic, not God's logic. God's thoughts are higher than our thoughts, and his understanding is infinitely higher than ours, which means inevitably that we, as finite, created human beings, cannot fully fathom it.

> For as the heavens are higher than the earth,
>   so are my ways higher than your ways
>   and my thoughts than your thoughts. (Isa. 55:9)

We can't fully understand it. It's as simple as that; it is beyond us. But that doesn't mean it's not true. Acts 4 sees nothing at all illogical in stating that God's enemies, in killing Jesus, were nevertheless doing exactly what God's sovereign hand had predestined to happen. They "were gathered together against your holy servant Jesus . . . to do whatever your hand and your plan had predestined to take place" (vv. 27–28). The Bible sees no logical problem with that, even if we do, because it is conversant with a higher, divine knowledge far beyond our finite, human understanding. We can't fully comprehend it. Of course we can't; if we could we would be divine ourselves! But we are not divine; we are human, and we just have to accept that fact, however humbling it is, along with the limitations that go with not being God.[12]

Now, you might be saying to yourself, "Well, that's very unsatisfactory!" Certainly a skeptic might say, "That's a typical Christian cop-out. It's just nonsense! You can't argue your logic, so you run off and take refuge in mystery, saying it is just beyond explanation." I heard Anthony Grayling, the atheist philosopher, saying exactly that on the radio recently: "Oh, yes, you Christians, you fly away off, and you take refuge in mystery." Richard Dawkins, too, says and writes very similar things.

So is that what we're doing in speaking this way about a higher logic, a "hidden wisdom of God" far above the "wisdom of men" that trumps even the greatest "wisdom of this age"? (see 1 Cor. 2:5–8).

No, that is not what we're doing. When we say that there are things beyond us that we cannot understand, we are expressing something called "humility." We are simply saying that we, as human beings, are not omniscient, all knowing; and we're not arrogant enough to assume that unless *we* can understand something absolutely and completely, then it can't possibly be true. By contrast, what atheists such as Anthony Grayling and Richard Dawkins and others seem to be saying is, "If it's beyond *my* understanding, beyond *my* powers of reasoning, then it can't possibly be real." I don't know about you, but there are lots of things beyond my understanding that are nevertheless true. I can't understand relativity theory, and I doubt if you can either. (There might be some reading this who can, but not very many!) I cannot understand the theory of general relativity, let alone special relativity, but I don't thereby totally reject it. I have got good reason to trust Albert Einstein and others like him, even though it is way beyond my level of mathematics and physics. I accept that there may well be a higher intelligence at work than mine.

Humility is something we recognize as necessary in all kinds of ways at all different levels in our lives. Just think of a young child who asks her mother for ice cream on a hot day. She knows her mother loves her. So she expects her mother to give her ice cream, and indeed, she has good grounds for this belief since she has experienced exactly this situation often before. It's very logical to her child-like mind. But if the little girl keeps on asking for more and more ice cream, there is going to come a time when Mother is going to say, "No, you can't have ice cream." At that point the child may get upset, perhaps even cry. "It's illogical!" says her little brain. "Why is Mommy not giving me ice cream anymore? Doesn't she love me?" It is beyond the child's logic, which says, "If one ice cream is good and two ice creams even better, why on earth is a third ice cream not better still and coming my way?"

Well, there's a higher logic at work than the child's limited reasoning—mother's logic. The mother has a loving, protective understanding that knows, despite her daughter's protests, that limitless ice cream, far from being loving indulgence, will very likely make her daughter sick in the short term and obese in the long term. (Thank goodness for mother's logic. Father's logic isn't always the same; it's usually good for an extra ice cream or two, especially if Dad gets to join in.)

Now, this same principle applies when it comes to our understanding of God. By definition, if God is God and we are creatures, his children, sometimes his good and perfect wisdom will seem, for us, totally impossible to fathom. It may seem illogical, as though all reason has broken down. In reality, it is simply a matter of our incomplete knowledge and limited experience in contrast to his complete knowledge and infinite experience.

We cannot be the arbiters of God's logic. Instead, we need simply to think about the Bible's unembarrassed handling of these matters and humbly seek to trust the divine wisdom that Scripture reveals to us. If we cannot understand all things, it doesn't mean they cannot be true, even though we cannot always see how one thing may be true at the same time as another. Sometimes we are told by somebody we trust completely that something which we ourselves can't properly fathom is really true. Surely the logical thing to do in such circumstances is to trust that we have good grounds to believe it is indeed true and accept it as true. Similarly, for the Christian believer, when the Bible tells us that two apparently contradictory things *are* nevertheless true, and when we have the personal assurance of the Lord Jesus Christ that all God's words can be trusted, we can trust him without needless doubt.

When you think about it, we have to do that in all kinds of different ways in our daily experience, based on far lesser authorities than the words of God. I was listening to a radio discussion recently about the great breakthrough in physics, when scientists finally understood that light is both a wave form and made up of particles. That was apparently inconceivable to people. I don't think I really understand it myself; how can light consist of particles and also be a wave? Perhaps you can understand and explain it. But the fact is that it took a long time for even exceptionally bright scientists to be able to grasp that apparent paradox, and it was a great breakthrough when they did. I still can't fathom it fully, but I believe it; planes fly in the air, and spaceships go to the moon, and other extraordinary things can happen because they are true.

Likewise, the Bible tells us, God is both wholly sovereign, and at the same time we, as human beings, are wholly responsible for our actions in relation to him. I can't fathom that fully, but I believe and trust Jesus Christ and his apostles enough to believe that it's true. We'll focus more specifically in a moment on how the Bible applies this higher wisdom of God's sovereignty to our thinking about our prayers. But first, let's think briefly about how it applies more generally in terms of the logic of the sovereignty of God in salvation.

The Logic of God's Sovereignty in Salvation

Prayer, as we've already seen, is simply one expression of salvation. Restoration of prayer is an integral part of the restoration of our true and right relationship with God, which is salvation—eternal life in the presence of God. So the question of how our prayers play a meaningful part in things with a sovereign God is really a subset of the question of our responsibility for faith if God is wholly sovereign. That bigger issue can often seem problematic. It's an apparent contradiction, because the Bible is very clear that both things are true.

First, the Bible is absolutely clear that we are responsible for our sins. We must repent, and we have a responsibility to do so in response to the command of the gospel. That was Jesus's repeated message right from the start of his earthly ministry: "From that time Jesus began to preach, saying, 'Repent, for the kingdom of heaven is at hand'" (Matt. 4:17). It was the apostles' message, likewise, after him: "Repent . . . in the name of Jesus Christ for the forgiveness of your sins," cried Peter on the day of Pentecost (Acts 2:38). All through the apostolic ministry the same refrain was heard: "Repent! Turn from your sins!" There is absolutely no doubt about that command.

Yet, second, the Bible is equally clear that we cannot do

this very thing that we are commanded to do unless God, by his sovereign power, should cause us to repent. Repentance is something that God alone can give. Acts 5:31 says that Jesus was raised so that God might "give repentance" and forgiveness to his people. Ephesians 2:1 is just as plain when Paul is describing the process of salvation. He says, "You were dead in your transgressions." Well, dead people cannot bring themselves to life, can they? They can't do anything. Only God's power can do that. As Jesus himself said, it is through his sovereign call alone that "the dead will hear the voice of the Son of God, and those who hear will live" (John 5:25). There is absolutely no doubt that true repentance comes only through the sheer sovereign call of God's saving grace.

From a biblical standpoint, both things are true. It's not *either* God is really sovereign, and therefore he must call people unto salvation, *or* we are really responsible and therefore must repent. The Bible is unambiguous; both are affirmed without doubt. God is sovereign, and we are responsible. A higher reasoning than the mere "wisdom of men" is at work.

That doesn't mean it is illogical. Nor does it mean that we can't grasp anything at all about how this can be so. In fact, we can. We can see how this works out, to a degree at least, even in our own experience of life, because the fact is that responsibility is not incompatible with authority; it actually flows from it. Notice that I am using the language of responsibility rather than of free will, which is a different thing altogether. Free will, in the sense of human beings being totally and utterly free (sometimes called "libertarian freedom") to do exactly and totally as they please against God's sovereign will, is not a biblical concept. That *would* be absolutely at odds with a truly sovereign God.

Human beings, according to the Bible, are wholly responsible for their actions, and that is not at all incompatible with God's sovereign authority. A drunk driver doesn't have free will. He is not free to drive with all his faculties. He is not free in that sense, but he does nevertheless bear full responsibility for his actions. If he kills someone, he cannot stand in the court and say, "Sorry, your honor, I was drunk, so I can't possibly be held responsible for this accident." That is laughable, isn't it? That's no defense; it is pleading guilty, and he is responsible precisely because he was drunk. He is responsible even though he doesn't have free will in the sense of complete libertarian freedom to drive with all due care and attention. He is responsible because, like absolutely everybody else on the roads, he is in a relationship with authority, in this case with the law of the land.

All true responsibility, when you think about it, actually presupposes a relationship of authority. It is authority that confers responsibility, and therefore also dignity and value, on people. If your boss gives you a task and says to you, "Now, look, John, I'm going to make you responsible for this," you don't say, "Oh, I can't possibly be held responsible for this because my boss has the authority." It's because he has the authority to make you responsible that you are therefore responsible. That's why you can be held accountable; you wouldn't be responsible at all unless he had the authority to make you so.

It is in this same way that the Bible talks about our responsibility before a sovereign God with respect to his sovereign salvation. Salvation begins with God. He is sovereign; he has all the authority, and therefore he makes us responsible to respond to his command. He makes us responsible to his call of salvation. God speaks his saving word, and we will express either submission to that word or rebellion against it. We will respond either with what the Bible calls "the obedience of faith"[13] or with the disobedience of unbelief, but either way we are fully responsible to God because he has sovereignly given us the responsibility to obey.

So the Bible's understanding of God's sovereignty in salvation is not an either/or reasoning, but a both/and reasoning, which means that we can never say, "Oh, if God's sovereign, I don't *need* to repent. If I'm elect, well, I'll be saved because God's sovereign." Nor can we ever say, "Oh, well, it's not my fault. I *can't* respond if I'm not elect, so how can God possibly hold me responsible?" No! Acts 17:30 tells us that God "commands all people everywhere to repent." His sovereign authority calls every single human being to account.

It should be no surprise, then, to discover that it is just the same when we think about prayer. We can never say,

"God is sovereign, so we never need to pray," or, "God is sovereign so there's no point in praying." No. Biblical logic says, "God is sovereign; therefore, not only *can* I pray but I *must* pray and I *will* pray. Just as it is both/and in the Bible's logic of God's sovereignty in our salvation, so it is similarly both/and when we think more specifically about the Bible's logic of the sovereignty of God and our prayer.

The Logic of God's Sovereignty in Prayer

First, let me deal with a very common, but I think quite an unhelpful, view of prayer. It's summed up by an aphorism that is quite common among evangelical Christians: "Prayer changes things." I am sure you have heard that often, and I have probably said it unthinkingly myself at times. It sounds good, of course, and like many aphorisms, there is some truth in it. But as so often with evangelical clichés, underneath this quite pious-sounding phrase there lurks a defective view of God, because it smacks of trying to persuade God to do something that he otherwise won't do. People repeating this phrase rather assume (and, in fact, sometimes assert quite plainly) that God won't work unless we pray, or (worse) God can't work unless we pray. Sometimes I've even heard people say, "God is helpless to do anything in this world unless his people are truly praying." That implies that God is, in fact, impotent without the help of our prayers, which really is quite blasphemous, when you think about it for more than a moment.

If you keep pushing in that direction, you end up with the god of what is called "open theism," a theological belief that God can't really know or control the future, because he is contingent on the choices that people make. Such thinking de-gods God. It flatly denies the witness of Scripture, reducing God to a being like the genie in Aladdin's lamp, dancing to our tune and at our beck and call. That view holds that God is not the sovereign Lord of the universe; rather, he cooperates with us to serve us, to answer our prayers. But if that were the case, the future would be dependent not on God but on us, because it's all about what we ask God to do. That's not biblical Christianity at all; in fact, it is simply paganism.

If we seriously take the whole of Scripture and its many constituent parts as a witness to God, we cannot possibly hold to this kind of view of our prayers changing and manipulating God, as though he were dependent upon our petitions. Indeed, reading just a few verses from Isaiah 46 blows this notion of a nonsovereign God completely out of the water:

> I am God, and there is no other;
>> I am God, and there is none like me,
> declaring the end from the beginning
>> and from ancient times things not yet done,
> saying, "My counsel shall stand,
>> and I will accomplish all my purpose,"
> calling a bird of prey from the east,

the man of my counsel from a far country.
I have spoken, and I will bring it to pass;
   I have purposed, and I will do it. (Isa. 46:9–11)

You could almost pick at random passages from the prophet Isaiah and from many other parts of Scripture that totally dispel any sense of this idea that God won't, or far worse, can't, do things without his people's prayers. It simply doesn't fit with the overwhelming biblical data. So if we mean by the phrase "Prayer changes things" that prayer takes control of God and his thoughts and his ways, I'm afraid that just won't do at all.

A much better dictum is this: "Prayer is thinking God's thoughts after him." I remember my father putting it to me like that when I was a young child,[14] and it really is a much healthier way of expressing the Bible's reasoning about prayer. It tells us that prayer is not a sort of cold, mathematical logic but a warm relational understanding. Remember, prayer is the audible witness of a real relationship with God, and the truth about prayer is that God the sovereign Lord invites us into a place of privileged partnership with him, a real partnership in his business, if you like. And that's what our prayers are. We follow after him, walking along with him, learning about his business and having a share in it.

We pray because we are God's sons, and as sons, we have come to share God's family business. That is what sons do; they share in the privilege of their birth into the family firm and therefore share the goals of the whole enterprise.

Well, in the gospel, God has revealed to us his great business, his great purpose of salvation for this world in Christ. Not only that, but he has granted us a part, a real share, in the ongoing concern of his family business. We have a part in Almighty God and Sons, Unlimited, you might say. We have shared ownership of it because he has given it to us and called us to be involved. Now, we could, I suppose, rebel against that whole concern. But that would be as bizarre as someone promoted to junior partner in a big firm devoting himself to working totally against the ethos of the firm, setting himself at odds with the senior partner. It's just ridiculous. The most natural thing, of course, is to throw everything into the vision, the ethos, and the goals of the company in which you have been made a partner.

That is just the way it is with us. God's big picture, his great sovereign salvation, will surely become *our* great concern as well, because having become his sons, we increasingly think his thoughts after him. We increasingly share his heart's desire and passion so that those things begin to fill our prayers, as we see exemplified in Paul's prayers in the New Testament. Read them in Ephesians 1 and 3, for example. There he prays that believers will grasp the dimensions of the greatness of God's salvation. He prays that there will be glory in the church in Christ Jesus forever. That is real Christian prayer; he is thinking God's thoughts after him. He is praying in line with God's purposes for all of history and for eternity. That doesn't exclude, of course, prayer for small things or personal things or specific things. The same Paul writes to the Philippians saying exactly that: bring *all* your requests before God. Don't be anxious about anything (Phil. 4:6). Nevertheless, even there in Philippians, the instruction about prayer is given in the context of having eyes set upon the great goal that is to come, the return of the Savior Jesus Christ from heaven. That is to be the context that colors their thinking. Real gospel prayer always does that, because real gospel prayer always thinks God's thoughts after him. It has God's goal in view.

That means we have to ask ourselves practical questions about where our prayer focus is. Whose thoughts are we thinking when we pray? In our church prayer meeting, is it *all* about small things—personal things, things to do with us and our present health or circumstances, or whatever else? Is that true in our personal prayers, in our family prayers? Or is it always, whatever we're praying for, undergirded by a focus on the great issues of Christ and his coming kingdom, on thinking God's thoughts after him?

It's not so much *what* we pray for, whether it's large or small things, but what motivates our prayer that really matters. We need to ask ourselves that. Is it all in line with the ethos, the great goal, of our Father's business, just as it was in Acts 4? Those early Christians, when faced with real and present threats and imprisonment, did not pray, "Hear their threats and keep us from further threats," though that is likely how we would be praying. "Hear their threats and keep us witnessing to the gospel of Jesus Christ"—that was their prayer. "May we keep on speaking the word boldly," they prayed (see vv. 23–29). That was their chief goal because they were thinking God's thoughts after him.

That is the sheer privilege of prayer, which is granted to us—to be involved in God's great purpose of salvation as partners in his family business, because he is sovereign, and because he will accomplish everything he has purposed by his grace. We have been given the inestimable privilege of being part of the team that will not only accomplish the purpose but also share in the glory.

Manchester United is probably the most famous football (soccer) team in the world, and Sir Alex Ferguson, their longest serving coach, who retired in 2013, one of the most successful, and admired, managers in the history of the game. In twenty-six years at the club, he won an astonishing thirty-eight trophies, including thirteen English Premier League and two European Champions League titles. During his reign only a brave man would have bet against Sir Alex Ferguson winning yet another championship. None doubted Sir Alex's sovereignty, authority, and control over Manchester United. He was, supremely, the great architect of victory.

Well, just imagine that it is the very end of the season, with just one more league game to play. Sir Alex Ferguson's team, Manchester United, is ten points ahead. They are unreachable, and the last game is against a club languishing at the bottom of the league. It will almost certainly be a goal fest for United. Now imagine he has chosen *you* to play alongside his galaxy of stars in that last game, to finish the league, to wear the medal, to lift the trophy.

That's just a faint analogy to the certain conquest in which God our Father has given us a part through our prayers. He has called us to join his team in a victory that is infinitely more certain. Remember Jesus's own words: "The harvest is plentiful, but the laborers are few; therefore pray earnestly to the Lord of the harvest to send out laborers into his harvest" (Matt. 9:37–38). Do you see what he's saying? The sovereign Lord has decreed that the harvest *is* plentiful, that there *shall be* a great harvest for his kingdom. He is sovereign in salvation. Therefore, says the Lord Jesus Christ, *we* are to pray earnestly to him, the Lord of the harvest, that *he* will send out laborers through whom that harvest, which he has decreed, will be accomplished. We are to pray to be aligned with his thoughts, with his wonderful, gracious, merciful thoughts, and by doing so become a part of the accomplishing of that great goal.

We pray because God is sovereign and because, as his sons, we share in the glory of that purpose for the world.

Can you imagine, after being picked to play in that trophy-winning team, turning round to Sir Alex Ferguson and saying, "No, I can't be bothered. It's already in the bag—everybody knows who's going to win. I'll not bother"? Of course, you wouldn't. You want to be on that pitch, and you want to hear that final whistle, having felt the sweat pouring off you and knowing the joy of playing. You want to hear the roar of the crowd as the final whistle approaches. You want to go up to the stand and get that medal and lift the trophy. You are thrilled at being a part of a historic victory, *even though you know* no other team in the league has got any possible chance of beating you. You want to be on the pitch.

That's why we pray. God wants us to be on his pitch, thinking his thoughts after him, playing our part in a certain, glorious victory, the bringing in of the kingdom of his Son. And the more we think his thoughts after him, the more we'll rejoice in talking about those thoughts with him, and with one another, in prayer.

So let's thank God that as Christian believers, we can pray. Our God truly is sovereign. If he were not, we couldn't pray at all.

Questions for Reflection or Discussion

1. Philip points out that God's sovereignty could be seen as either a problem for prayer or a reason for prayer. Why might God's sovereignty make us not want to pray? Why is God's sovereignty, in fact, a reason why we should pray? In which light do you usually see God's sovereignty—as an obstacle or an impetus for prayer?

2. What distinction does Philip make between free will and responsibility? How does that differentiation change the way you think about God's sovereign authority over people and the role that individuals play in the process of salvation? How is

our responsibility an expression of the dignity and value God places on us?

3. In what areas of life do you submit to someone else's superior wisdom, possibly without even realizing it? Ultimately God's sovereignty and our responsibility are an apparent contradiction that our finite minds cannot fully reconcile. What helps you come to terms with not fully understanding the relationship between God's sovereignty and human responsibility? How might thinking of God's sovereignty as something we should logically submit to because of his superior wisdom change your prayer life?

4. Why is it unbiblical to say that "prayer changes things"? How does this phrase diminish God's power?

5. In what ways is prayer "thinking God's thoughts after him"? How have you experienced this phenomenon in your own life? How does this idea inform and flesh out the relational nature of prayer? Does thinking of prayer in these terms make you long for prayer or not want to bother with it?

6. How can you tell whether you are thinking God's thoughts after him when you pray? How can you discern the motivation behind your prayers? Do you often ask yourself what motivates your prayers?

If you abide in me, and my words abide in you, ask whatever you wish, and it will be done for you. By this my Father is glorified, that you bear much fruit and so prove to be my disciples. As the Father has loved me, so have I loved you. Abide in my love. If you keep my commandments, you will abide in my love, just as I have kept my Father's commandments and abide in his love. These things I have spoken to you, that my joy may be in you, and that your joy may be full.

John 15:7–11

4

We Pray Because
We Have the Spirit of God

We pray because God is a speaking God. The relationship we were created for was ruined by our sin, but God did not retreat into silence. He went on speaking into his world words of promise, reaching their zenith at last in the person of Jesus Christ his Son. To him we turn in faith for our salvation, a faith vocalized in trusting prayer, the unequivocal evidence of "the life of God in the soul of man."[15] And because God has adopted us into his family, we have come to share the privilege of intimate relationship that Jesus, God's perfect Son, has with his Father and our Father. We pray because in Christ we too are sons of God. Moreover, because we are sons, we are brought into real partnership with the sovereign God to think his thoughts after him and participate, through our prayers, in his purposes of eternal glory.

I want to think a little more in this final chapter about

the implications of the subject we explored in the previous chapter, namely, prayer that is truly aligned with God's sovereign purpose in his gospel. It is important because, obviously, God's purpose, if he is truly sovereign, is sure and certain. If we pray in line with God's sovereign purpose, truly thinking his thoughts after him, we are praying in alignment with God's goals. And if that is so, then of course those prayers must be answered because God will surely achieve his own purpose.

Certainly that is what Jesus himself tells us. Because this is true, we are to pray confidently in faith. He says to his disciples, "Whatever you ask in prayer, you will receive, if you have faith" (Matt. 21:22). He puts it slightly differently, but certainly no less clearly or definitively, several times in the "Farewell Discourse," as we call it, where Jesus teaches his closest disciples in the upper room just prior to his crucifixion. "If you ask anything in my name, I will do it," says Jesus (John 14:14). "Whatever you ask of the Father in my name, he will give it to you" (John 16:23). "If you abide in me, and my words abide in you, ask whatever you wish, and it will be done for you" (John 15:7).

Those are very definite statements, aren't they? There is no doubt about it; they are absolute and unqualified. Because that is true, they can be, and alas they often have been, abused. The definite nature of Jesus's words has been misused by some Christians as though Jesus was saying we have carte blanche to use his name in prayer as little more than a mantra, or a lucky charm, whenever we really want to get what we desire from God in prayer. But, once again, that is to totally misunderstand the gospel. The gospel isn't a lucky charm to give us what we want from God. It is quite the reverse; it is God's grace and mercy at work to give God what he desires from our lives. It is how God does what he wants to change us to be like him through our union with his Son, the Lord Jesus. The gospel is all about God's aligning us with his sovereign purposes, not our aligning God with our selfish purposes through our prayers.

Only the Holy Spirit Can Make Us Real Pray-ers

Only the Holy Spirit can make us real pray-ers. That's why John 15:7 is so important. According to Jesus, prayer that exhibits real faith, prayer that is genuinely in his name, comes from those who abide in Christ, that is, from people in whom his words abide.

The whole of the Upper Room Discourse of Jesus with his disciples centers on how that can be. How will Jesus's words abide in his people after he leaves them on earth and ascends to his Father in heaven? The answer, of course, is through the ministry of the Holy Spirit.

What Jesus teaches his closest disciples, the apostles, in the upper room is of seminal importance. Jesus says to them, "I will not leave you as orphans; I will come to you. . . . The Helper, the Holy Spirit . . . will teach you all things and bring to your remembrance all that I have said to you." The Holy Spirit's ministry will be to lead the apostles into "all the truth" (see John 14:16, 18, 25–26; 16:13).

Notice that Jesus is speaking there explicitly to his apostles, not just vaguely to his followers in general, and certainly not directly to you and me today; the Spirit cannot bring to our remembrance things Jesus spoke to us during his earthly ministry. His words belong to a unique moment in history, and they concern the once-for-all transition into the post-resurrection, post-Pentecost, New Testament era of the church. Jesus is explaining how his church will know his Word and abide in his Word, how those who come afterward will have his commands and keep them and thus know him and love him, and be loved by Jesus and his Father, and so come to belong to them. People all over the world ever afterward will be able to come to him and abide in him only because they will have access through the Holy Spirit's ministry, as Peter later puts it, to "the commandment of the Lord and Savior through your apostles" (2 Pet. 3:2). The Holy Spirit will reveal *to the apostles* all the church needs to know of God's sovereign purposes of grace for his kingdom until Jesus comes again in glory. The Holy Spirit "will declare to you [the apostles] the things that are to come," said Jesus (John 16:13). And Christ's followers who love Jesus, he says, will keep his word through the apostolic ministry, so that the Father and the Son will come to make their home with them through the Holy Spirit. That is how his people are going to know Jesus's words and how his words are truly going to abide in them—he is going to send them his Holy Spirit.

As New Testament Christians today, we abide in Christ if his words—words that reveal his sovereign purposes—abide in us through the ministry of the Holy Spirit dwelling within us. Therefore, to say that we pray in Jesus's name and that we pray with real faith is simply another way of saying that we pray in the Holy Spirit. So we can be confident in prayer because, as Paul says to us in Romans 8:26–27, "the Spirit helps us in our weakness. For we do not know what to pray for as we ought, but the Spirit himself intercedes for us with groanings too deep for words. . . . The Spirit intercedes for the saints *according to the will of God.*" Through the Holy Spirit we are enabled to pray according to God's will, in line with his good and perfect and acceptable will.

We pray because we have God's Holy Spirit, who alone can enable us to pray in Jesus's name and with real faith. To speak about prayer is to speak about the ministry of the Holy Spirit of Jesus within people. It is all about his ministry *for* us, his ministry *in* us, and his ministry *to* us. I want to focus on those three things in particular, because they are so important in helping us understand the difference between real Christian prayer—in which we should be utterly confident and which will be answered—and prayer that is just presumptuous, which won't be answered because it isn't actually Christian prayer at all. The sobering truth is, there are lots of pagan prayers, albeit dressed up in pious Christian language, in the Christian church, which is why we really need to understand the difference. We need to be clear.

The Holy Spirit's Sovereign Work for Us

The Holy Spirit alone can enable us to pray in Jesus's name because it is his sovereign work to confer the name of Jesus upon us, bringing us into the family of God. That is how we receive the adoption as sons that enables us to call God "Father."

The name of God is vitally important throughout the Old Testament. God's people have always been marked as those who have the privilege of knowing the name of Almighty God. To his own people he has revealed his personal name, his covenant name, YHWH, Jehovah, or Yahweh (translated LORD, in small capital letters, in our Bibles).[16] God's people bear that name, which is why the third commandment is so important. That commandment instructs God's people that they must never bear that name in vain, by which is meant casually or in an unworthy manner. God's name is bound up with the very identity of his people, and they are to honor it always.

We are never to bring God's name into disrepute. There are certain school rules for students who are required to wear a school uniform. If a student is caught misbehaving out of uniform, when school isn't in session, that's really not a huge issue for the school, but if a student misbehaves while wearing his school blazer, that is very different. It becomes a real issue, because the name of the school is brought into disrepute. Similarly, football players are fined by their club or league for bringing the game into disrepute if they behave dishonorably, which all too often they do. I am sure it is just the same concerning your workplace. Wherever you work, there are all kinds of rules about bringing your company, or your employer, into disrepute. If you do certain things, you will lose your job. You can't bring the good name of the company into disrepute with impunity.

God himself has conferred an extraordinary honor upon his people in allowing them to bear his name. In Numbers 6, speaking of what we call the Aaronic blessing, God says that Aaron the high priest and all his successors will bless the people by putting the Lord's name upon them: "So shall they put my name upon the people of Israel, and I will bless them" (v. 27). It is the sovereign work of the Spirit of God to confer his name of blessing upon his people. That is the wonder of the blessing of new birth. To all who "believed in his name," says John, "he gave the right to become children of God, who were born, not of blood nor of the will of the flesh nor of the will of man, but of God" (John 1:12–13). Jesus is explicit when speaking to Nicodemus: "Unless one is born of water and the Spirit, he cannot enter the kingdom of God" (John 3:5). Only those who are born from above, who are born of the Holy Spirit, who are reborn by adoption into God's family—only these can bear the family name.

That is why Jesus came, so that through his death and resurrection, the promised Holy Spirit would be poured out upon all peoples, that there might be from every tribe and tongue and people and nation those redeemed in Christ and reborn in the Spirit to belong to the family of God. That is what Peter proclaimed on the day of Pentecost. The risen Jesus, "being therefore exalted at the right hand of God, and having received from the Father the promise of the Holy Spirit, he has poured out this that you yourselves are seeing and hearing" (Acts 2:33). The one Aaron foreshadowed, our Great High Priest, having completed all sacrifice for sin forever, and having ascended to the right hand of God on high (Heb. 10:10–14), has blessed his people by sending his Holy Spirit to put his name upon his people forever.

The Holy Spirit's work for us is to bring us to new birth as the children of God who bear Jesus's name because we are united to him. That is why we can be real pray-ers, people who are able to pray to God. We can call out to God our heavenly Father because we pray in Jesus's name. Prayer is all about the Holy Spirit's work for us.

THE HOLY SPIRIT'S SUBJECTIVE WITNESS IN US

The New Testament tells us that the Holy Spirit is also a *witness in us*.

The Spirit of God removes our blindness; he opens up

and takes away the hardness of our hearts and turns our eyes to Jesus our Savior that we might see him and subjectively cast everything upon him for salvation. The apostle Paul says that having received the Spirit of adoption as sons, we cry out, "Father!" It is the Spirit himself who bears witness with our spirits that we are sons of God (Rom. 8:15–16). So through the sovereign call of God, through the sovereign work of the Spirit for us, the life-giving power of the gospel comes to us; and through the same Spirit, we subjectively answer that call by faith as we respond personally to God. "Because you are sons, God has sent the Spirit of his Son into our hearts, crying, 'Abba! Father!'" (Gal. 4:6).

Once again, here is the both/and reasoning of the Bible—both God's sovereignty and our responsibility in our response. So the Holy Spirit's working in our salvation involves both a sovereign work for us and his witness in and with us in our subjective response to God. There is no incompatibility between his work and our response because both God's call and our response are the work of the same Holy Spirit of God. We see this when Paul was preaching in Antioch of Pisidia, at which time, Luke tells us, "as many as were appointed to eternal life believed" (Acts 13:48). Notice the careful clarity of Luke's words. They were *appointed* to eternal life, called by the sovereign work of the Spirit of God *for* them. But it came about as they *believed*, responding through the Spirit's work *in* them, witnessing with them and calling out to God, "Abba! Father!" Jesus shows the same in John 6: "All that the Father *gives me* will come to me" (v. 37). A sovereign work. Then he immediately says, "This is the will of my Father, that everyone who looks on the Son and *believes* in him should have eternal life" (v. 40).

So the response of faith that we make to God's call is also the work of the Holy Spirit. The same Spirit of adoption who is sovereignly at work to enable us to pray in Jesus's name also enables us to pray with real faith and feeling through his saving witness in our hearts, which bears witness with our spirit that we are sons of God. Prayer is simply the audible form of this response of faith. As John Calvin starkly put it, "Prayer is the chief exercise of our faith." And if that is so, if prayer really is the call of hearts united to Jesus by his Holy Spirit, then prayer made through the Spirit in Jesus's name is praying Jesus's prayers after him, just as we think his thoughts after him. That is why we can be certain that such prayer will always be answered.

Because through faith the Holy Spirit makes us into real pray-ers, and because real pray-ers pray Jesus's prayers after him, well, it must be obvious that they will be prayers God will answer.

"Now, hang on a second!" you say. "It's all very well to say that the prayers of real pray-ers praying in the Spirit and in line with the purpose of Jesus will be answered. I can follow the theological argument, and I may even be convinced by it. But how does that work in my life? How do I know exactly what the will of God is about something?

How can I, when I'm praying, be absolutely sure that my plan and purpose in prayer is totally aligned with the plan and purpose of the Lord Jesus Christ?"

That's where we find difficulty, isn't it? The answer to our difficulty lies once again in the same place, or rather, in the same person—the Holy Spirit.

Only the Holy Spirit Can Make Our Prayers Real

Just as only the Holy Spirit can make us into real pray-ers, so only the Holy Spirit can make our prayers real Christian prayers, that is, prayers that truly are in line with the sovereign will and purpose of God. The Spirit leads us in prayer that will be aligned with that sovereign purpose through his ministry to us through the Scriptures.

THE HOLY SPIRIT'S SCRIPTURAL WORD TO US

If through the Spirit's *work for us* we are born anew as sons of God who can truly pray in Jesus's name, and if through his *witness in us* we really can cry out in faith to our Father, then it is through the Holy Spirit's *word to us* that we can be totally confident about the will and purpose of God in all things and therefore pray with confident faith and full assurance in all our prayers.

Isn't that a massive relief? We can pray confidently and with absolute certainty that we are praying in line with God's Holy Spirit because he is our personal assistant. He has put it all in writing for us, so we do not have to guess what God's sovereign will and purpose is and so we shall never forget it. It is all there in black and white.

I don't know if you, like me, are terribly forgetful. It used to be that I had the ability to forget the things I wanted to forget (such as chores my wife might ask me to do on a Saturday morning while I am reading the newspaper) and to remember the things I wanted to remember (such as the time that coverage of the six-nations rugby match starts). Now, alas, I'm beginning to forget much more indiscriminately, and I need to write things down; otherwise I will forget everything.

I suppose I probably have more things to think about all at once than I used to—too many, perhaps—and I often do forget things. The truth is that my work would be a total shambles were it not for the fact that I'm not on my own; in God's goodness he has given me a personal assistant called Alison to help me in the church. And what Alison does for me very frequently is write things down. A little note appears on the front of my order of service on Sundays just to make sure I remember what I've wanted to say. Alison's notes appear constantly, mainly in my e-mail inbox but also through the mail. Again and again she has written things down so that I will remember.

That is what the Holy Spirit is to us: a helper or comforter, as Jesus calls him. "Paraclete" is the transliterated Greek term, and it refers to somebody who comes alongside to help and to remember. The Holy Spirit, our personal helper, has enabled us to be confident that we know and remember by writing it down for us. He has written it in the Scriptures of the Old and New Testaments.

That is what Jesus said in John 14–16. He told the apostles that when he ascended to heaven, the Holy Spirit would come and lead them (he was speaking directly to the apostles, remember) into all the truth. They, in turn, with all his authority and through his inspiration and control, wrote it down for us so that we who now possess the whole of the Scriptures, both the Old and the New Testaments, can know what the clear and certain will and purpose of God is about everything that really matters in our lives. When we forget or get confused, we come back and open up these words from the Holy Spirit and read what he's written to us so that we are not confused anymore.

That's why Peter could say that the church has been given "all things that pertain to life and godliness, through the knowledge of him who has called us to his own glory" (2 Pet. 1:3). He is talking about the Scriptures. It is these Scriptures and the great and precious promises they contain, breathed out by God's Spirit himself, that are, as Paul likewise reminds us, able to make us wise for salvation through faith in Jesus Christ. They are able to teach us, to rebuke us, and to correct our thinking and so lead us on with certainty in a life of faith and righteousness (2 Tim. 3:15–16). The Holy Spirit has written his words to us so that we should have everything we need for our life of faith, which includes our prayers.

That is what Jesus said in John 15:7 about the prayers of those who abide in him, which will surely be answered. If we abide in him, our prayers will be aligned with his will, and we will abide in him (and therefore in his will) if *his words abide in us*, just as we will abide in his love if we keep his commandments, obeying *his words* (v. 10). Jesus's words, which are ours through the Scriptures, are for remembering and obeying—for abiding in.

Back to the question, "How do we pray with confidence that we are praying in the Spirit, that we're praying in God's will?" We know the answer now, don't we? It's simple: we pray in line with the clear revealed will of God's Holy Spirit in Scripture. We listen to the Spirit's words to us. That's just so plain all through the New Testament when you start to see it. Read Ephesians 6, and you will see that Paul includes prayer as part of the gospel armor; it is part of standing firm in the gospel, of trusting that what God has said is true. He writes, "Take . . . the sword of the Spirit, which is the word of God, praying at all times in the Spirit" (Eph. 6:17–18). Do you see what he's saying?

Some people speak of "praying in the Spirit" as if it were some kind of strange mystical thing, different from ordinary prayer. "Nonsense!" says Paul. It's just praying in line with God's will as revealed in his words in the Scriptures. God's Word reveals God's will from his Spirit. So when we pray, if it is real prayer, we're simply asking God to bring our lives and other people's lives into line with his sovereign purposes as they are revealed to us in the gospel of our Lord Jesus Christ in the Scriptures.

Those sovereign purposes are absolutely clear to Christians in terms of the ultimate outcome. We know that one day, every knee will bow to the Lord Jesus Christ, and there will be a great multitude that no one can number from every tribe and language and nation, loving and serving the Lord Jesus in a reborn world. That's made clear in Scripture, which is why Jesus says we can pray with absolute certainty, "Lord, your kingdom come," and know that God will answer that prayer. We can therefore pray also for many things that will serve that purpose, which we are commanded to do in Scripture.

We are commanded by Jesus in Matthew 9:38 to pray that the Lord would send out workers into his harvest field (and we should take it as a corollary that if we pray for that, we must also be willing to be part of that mission by *being* workers in that harvest field). We are to pray for the world, Paul says in 1 Timothy 2:1–8, for those who need the gospel and for the conditions necessary for the gospel to spread— peace and freedom. We are to pray often, Paul says, for the gospel itself, for its proclamation, for its progress, that it would run forth and have free course and glorify the Lord Jesus Christ. We know that we can pray for all these things. We are commanded to; it is the clear will and purpose of

God through his Spirit's words to us. And God must answer those prayers, because he authored them.

Of course, there are precise details about God's purposes that aren't revealed to us in Scripture, things, I guess, that we don't need to know, things perhaps we're better off not knowing. We don't know God's secret will in his sovereign electing grace—exactly whom God is calling, exactly how many there will be in any place. But we are commanded to preach the gospel to all and to pray to that end. We don't know exactly when Jesus will return. In fact, Jesus tells us plainly that we can't know, so we mustn't keep asking. But we are commanded very clearly to be ready for that coming, whenever it will be, and to work gladly for the master so we won't be found wanting when he does come. Surely, therefore, we should pray to that end: "Lord, help me to be ready for your coming." That is a prayer Jesus will answer. I am not told in the Bible if I'll live to see my fiftieth birthday or my ninety-fifth, nor are you told when you'll be taken home to be with the Lord. We are not told in the Scriptures which of us is going to lose our job this year, nor are we told whether we should do this job or that job, or marry this person or that person (unless we're already married, as I am, in which case I am told clearly not to try to marry anyone else!).

We are told some interesting things, however, such as in 1 Thessalonians 4:3, where we see it is God's will always that we should be holy; and in 1 Thessalonians 5:18 that it's God's will that we should be joyful and thankful in all circumstances. How many times, though, have you prayed with assurance, asking God to make you thankful and holy, in comparison to the number of times you've prayed and asked God to tell you whether you should do this job or that job or marry this person or that person?

There are many things in the Bible that we don't know for sure. But the real pray-er of faith can pray confidently, "Lord, fulfill your purposes among us today. Lord, fulfill your purposes for your glory in my life this coming week." You can know for certain that those things are God's will for you and your life.

You can also pray like this: "Lord, if it be your will, may I be spared to serve you till I'm ninety-five." *If it be your will*. It's not a lack of faith to pray that way, which is very important to know, especially when you're praying for the healing of somebody you love who has cancer or for a definitive resolution of some difficult situation you're involved in. It can't be wrong to pray with some uncertainty about such things, to pray, "Lord, if it be your will." It can't be wrong, even though some people would tell you that it *is* wrong and that the reason you are not getting the answers to your prayers is that you are not praying with enough faith. But it simply can't be wrong to pray, "Lord, if it be your will," if we are praying for something that God has not seen fit to reveal certainly and clearly in the Scriptures— the very Scriptures in which he says he has given us every single thing we need for life and godliness until his coming. Just to pray on and on and "claim faith" simply isn't faith at all, if it's claiming something that God's Holy Spirit has not promised to us clearly through his Word. The Spirit of God in us cannot bear false witness. To attempt to drum up lots of faith in order to be sure that God will answer our prayer is self-deception. Actually, it's a terrible thing—it's idolatry. It's making up a false god and calling it the true God. It's what Aaron did with the golden calf. "Here's your god. Worship him, pray to this god and look for the answers that you want!" No!

We do that if we pray presumptuously for something God hasn't promised us and that we can't be certain about. It doesn't matter how fervent our prayer is. In fact, it is Jesus himself who says that often the more fervent the prayer, the more pagan it is. As we noted earlier, that's what the pagans do, and we are not to emulate them. We are to pray like this: "Hallowed be your name. Your will be done." That was how Jesus prayed in Gethsemane. "Let this cup pass from me, but if it cannot, then your will be done." Not our will, not our assessment of what God would want and what God ought to do, but, "Your will be done because my heart's desire is for what you have revealed to be your purpose, the glory of your kingdom, and because I have faith and I trust the Lord Jesus Christ to know best how to accomplish his will in my life, even though I might have ideas of my own a lot of the time."

That's real prayer—prayer filled with the Holy Spirit—on the lips of our Lord Jesus himself. Jesus is the real prayer. But his Holy Spirit will make our prayers real too, if we'll be guided in them by all his words to us through the Scriptures.

We pray because we have God's Holy Spirit, and that means we really can trust Jesus's plain and simple words: "If you abide in me, and my words abide in you, ask whatever you wish, and it will be done for you."

That's what Jesus means, and that's how we should pray.

Questions for Reflection or Discussion

1. Philip writes that "the gospel isn't a lucky charm to give us what we want from God. . . . It is God's grace and mercy at work to give God what he desires from our lives." Which of these two definitions of the gospel is more in line with how you usually pray? What kinds of prayers does someone pray if they think of the gospel as aligning God with their own purposes? What kinds of prayers does someone pray if they think of the gospel as aligning each of us with God's sovereign purposes?

2. The Holy Spirit works for us to bring us into God's family. How does our adoption into God's family enable us to be true pray-ers? Is this work of the Spirit something you are aware of as you pray, or something that you should be aware of? Why or why not?

3. Philip writes, "Through the sovereign call of God, through the sovereign work of the Spirit for us, the life-giving power of the gospel comes to us; and through the same Spirit we subjectively answer that call by faith as we respond personally to God. 'Because you are sons God has sent the Spirit of his Son into our hearts crying, "Abba! Father!"' (Gal. 4:6)." How does the Holy Spirit's work in you help you to pray? What does the Holy Spirit do for you as you pray that you are not able to do on your own? How have you experienced his help in prayer?

4. In what ways do you agree or disagree with John Calvin's assertion that "prayer is the chief exercise of our faith"?

5. Is it easy or difficult for you to pray, "If it be your will"? What hinders you from praying in this way? What are the comforts and blessings available to those who pray in this way?

6. How can you know God's will so that you can pray his thoughts after him? Are there things you have prayed for or are praying for about which God has not revealed his will? What revealed biblical truth can inform your prayers in those matters to align your heart with God's?

Notes

1. Derek Thomas, "Only a Prayer Meeting!," *Banner of Truth* (October 1989): 15–16.
2. Graeme Goldsworthy, *Prayer and the Knowledge of God* (Leicester, UK: Inter-Varsity, 2003). Some of the key themes I have taken up in these studies owe a great deal to Graeme Goldsworthy's insights in chaps. 2–5 of this volume, and I acknowledge his help freely and gratefully. I encourage those who want to dig deeper to read his book, a rich resource I warmly commend.
3. "Word dominates the notion of God creating and communicating with people." Ibid., 21.
4. This is why a "covenant of creation" is sometimes spoken of, since the very act of God's creation by his word necessarily creates a relationship between himself and all that he has made, a relationship with the covenant God.
5. Perhaps among his least-known works, *Out of the Silent Planet*, *Perelandra* (*Voyage to Venus*), and *That Hideous Strength* are well worth reading if you haven't done so, or rereading them if you have.
6. See esp. Rom. 5:16–19.
7. See also Isa. 24:5; Hos. 6:7; 8:1; Heb. 9:15 for the language of transgression of God's covenant with man.
8. The high point is described in 1 Kings 10, with the kings of the earth seeking Solomon's wisdom, but the rot sets in immediately as the sad story of chapter 11 relates.
9. *Forever* is one of the great words of the book of Hebrews.

10. "Our sonship is not a gender issue; it is a status issue. Outside of Christ men are no closer to being sons of God than are women. In Christ our gender does not affect our standing with God either way. We are all one in Christ because we all share what belongs to him in his standing as Son of God, the acceptable human being before God." Goldsworthy, *Prayer and the Knowledge of God*, 43.

11. I am using the words *logical* and *illogical* in this chapter not in the narrow and formal philosophical sense (to do with principles governing correct or reliable inference) but rather in the colloquial way we use *logic* to mean "understanding," that which makes sense to us, understandable and reasoned thought and argument, as distinguished from unreasonable irrationality; or what seems possible over against impossibility to our minds.

12. Refusal to let God be God and the urge to usurp the place of God is the very essence of sin, as the account of Genesis 3 makes graphically plain, along with the inevitable and terrible implications of that attitude.

13. Notice this careful emphasis in the "bookends" of Paul's letter to the Romans (1:5; 16:26). Throughout the letter Paul usually uses the shorthand "faith" and "unbelief," but sometimes "obedience" and "disobedience" (e.g., 10:16, 21; 11:30; 15:18).

14. Graeme Goldsworthy uses this same phrase also. *Prayer and the Knowledge of God*, 61.

15. To use that fine phrase from the title of the book by Henry Scoughal, the seventeenth-century divine.

16. Ex. 3:15 focuses on this revelation of the name of YHWH to Moses at the burning bush, when God identifies himself as the God of the patriarchs, while in Ex. 33:19ff. it is in proclaiming his name, YHWH, to Moses that God reveals his character as merciful and gracious, slow to anger and abounding in steadfast love and faithfulness.

General Index

Aaronic blessing, 89
Abraham, 35–36
adoption, 51–58, 61–62, 88
apostles, priority of prayer, 12
ascension, 11

Bunyan, John, 15

Calvin, John, 92
communication, 26
covenant relationship, 23, 27–28, 44
creation, 22–29

early church, 63, 77
eternal life, 91

faith, 35–36, 52, 83, 87, 92
fall, 43–44
family prayers, 77
free will, 71

God, fellowship with, 14, 41–42;
      glory of, 79; hearing prayers,
      56–57; image of, 24–26; name
      of, 88–89, 104; right relation-
      ship with, 69–70; sovereignty
      of, 62–80, 91; speaking into
      creation, 22–29; status before,
      52–53; verbal communion with,

29, 32–33, 43; will of, 99; Word
      of, 96–98
Goldsworthy, Graeme, 103–4
gospel, 50–58, 77
grace, 14, 34–35

heaven, 28
Holy Spirit, 11, 48, 85–101
human dignity, 71
human nature, 26
human responsibility, 69–73, 91
humility, 65–66

idolatry, 100

Jesus, abiding in, 96; death and res-
      urrection of, 90; habit of prayer,
      12–13; kingdom work of, 79;
      praying in the name of, 84–85;
      responding to, 36–37, 42–43;
      temptation of, 46–47; as true
      Son of God, 43–49
justification, 52–53

Lewis, C. S., 42
Lord's Prayer, 13
Luther, Martin, 14–15

marriage, 27, 30–31
Mount of Olives, 13

Scripture Index

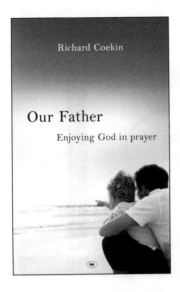

related titles from IVP

Our Father
Enjoying God in Prayer
Richard Coekin

ISBN: 978-1-84474-393-3
192 pages, paperback

'Our Father in heaven, Hallowed be your name ...'

When Jesus' disciples asked him for help with prayer, he gave them a beautifully simple but spiritually profound outline known as the Lord's Prayer. This utterly extraordinary prayer has been cherished by Christians everywhere and always. In it, our Saviour has brilliantly summarized the kinds of requests that God most delights to answer.

Jesus knew that, when we struggle to pray, we need, far more than techniques and challenges, a fresh appreciation of God. We need to glimpse his magnificent character and plans. As we see the Father described in Jesus' prayer, we find ourselves lifted in wonder to delight in him. Our cold hearts are warmed and our stifled tongues released to pray. The Lord's Prayer, and so this book, is all about enjoying God.

Says the author, *'I find the Lord's Prayer exhilarating. It has been a lifeline from God, dragging my proud heart to him. I couldn't survive without it.'*

Available from your local Christian bookshop or **www.thinkivp.com**

Inter-Varsity Press

For more information about IVP
and our publications visit
www.ivpbooks.com

Get regular updates at **ivpbooks.com/signup**
Find us on **facebook.com/ivpbooks**
Follow us on **twitter.com/ivpbookcentre**

Inter-Varsity Press, a company limited by guarantee registered in England and Wales, number 05202650. Registered office IVP Bookcentre, Norton Street, Nottingham NG7 3HR, United Kingdom. Registered charity number 1105757.